# ENGLISH TOPIARY GARDENS

# ·ENGLISH TOPIARY GARDENS·

## ETHNE CLARKE

◆

## GEORGE WRIGHT

*Clarkson N. Potter, Inc./Publishers*
DISTRIBUTED BY CROWN PUBLISHERS, INC., NEW YORK

Published by Clarkson N. Potter, Inc., 225 Park Avenue South, New York, New York 10003
Published in Great Britain by George Weidenfeld and Nicolson Ltd.
CLARKSON N. POTTER, POTTER, and colophon are trademarks of Clarkson N. Potter, Inc.
Manufactured in Italy
Library of Congress Cataloging-in-Publication Data

ISBN 0–517–56736–9

10 9 8 7 6 5 4 3 2 1

**Library of Congress Cataloging-in-Publication Data**

Clarke, Ethne.
English topiary gardens.

1. Topiary work.     2. Gardens, English.     I. Title
SB462.C564     1988     715'.1'0942     87–32895
ISBN 0–517–56736–9

*Half-title page* Manor House, Great Cheverell, Wiltshire
*Title page* Rangeworthy, Avon
*Overleaf* Arley Hall, Cheshire

# ACKNOWLEDGEMENTS

George and I would like to thank the following people for allowing us into their gardens to photograph their topiary and for taking the time to accompany us, and for providing masses of information and inspiration.

The Marchioness of Salisbury, Lord and Lady Ashbrook and the Hon. Michael Flower, Lady Cooke, Sir Edward and Lady Thompson, Mr and Mrs H. Bagot, Mr Christopher Lloyd, Mrs Rosemary Verey, Mr David Masters, Mr David Beaumont, Mr Tom Acton, Mr Christopher Crowther, Mrs Camfield, Mr N.G.J. Booker, Mrs Robinson, Mr S. Ponsillo, head gardener at Orchards, Mrs E.M. Randall, Mr G.W. Adams, Mr C.C. Houghton, Mr Ian Fairservice, Mrs Mary Biddulph, Mrs Clutton-Brock, Mrs A. Voaden, Mr D. Flowers, Mr and Mrs Desmond Heyward, Mr and Mrs Peter Ward, Mr and Mrs Alistair Macleod Matthews, Mr and Mrs Peregrine Palmer, Mrs Basil Feilding, Miss Phyllis Dodd, Mrs Mary Oliver, Mr and Mrs R. Lucy, Mr and Mrs John Pudge, Mr Christopher Rowley, Mr and Mrs N.G.K. Dawes, Mr Newman, Mrs Houghton, Mr and Mrs R.N. Burton, Mr and Mrs Randle Brooks, Mr and Mrs John Makepeace, Mr Gunton, Mr W.S. Norman, Mrs Barbara Weston, Mr Brian Fairchild, Mr Ruben Smith, Mr Adrian Powell, Mrs Fielding, Mr R. Heathman, Mrs Basil Barlow, Mrs Betty Mallam, Mr D.G.W. Barham, Mr Richard Winch, Mr Osborn, Mrs Oliver Brooke, Mr B. Halstead of the Oaksmere Free House, Brome, nr Eye, Suffolk, Hever Castle and Gardens, nr Edenbridge, Kent and the Administrators and Head Gardeners of the National Trust properties featured. Our special thanks to Margaret W. Hemmings, the National Trust organiser of the Biddulph Grange Garden Appeal; donations for the garden rescue may be sent to her and visits arranged through her at Grange Road, Biddulph, Stoke-on-Trent, ST8 7SD. Many of the gardens featured are open to the public at specified times. For example, Parnham House is open from April 1 to October 31 each Wednesday, Sunday and Bank Holiday Monday from 10–5. Opening dates and times for other properties can be found in the guide books of the National Gardens Scheme, Historic Houses, Castles and Gardens, and the *National Trust Handbook*. Please check with these guides before visiting.

We are especially grateful to all the topiary-loving gardeners who have gone before us, including the late Brigadier Oliver G. Brooke, whose passion for clipped bushes made this book possible.

# CONTENTS

# THE GRAND MANNER

Dinosaur footprints cast in the primal ooze, fossilized fronds and lumps of petrified wood help to create an image of our earth in its juvenile stages. All the various stages of mankind's development, our achievements and failures have been scrutinised over the centuries, the evidence examined through the common looking-glass of any number of scientific disciplines. So what remains of gardens? Our earliest creative urges were exercised in subduing the wildness of nature; we soon learned the advantages of the ordered cultivation of fruits, herbs and grains. It seems that it was only a short step from functional to amenity horticulture, and the birth of the decorative garden.

Visual records: tomb paintings and manuscript illuminations, for example, supplemented by written accounts and the wonders of modern archaeological method have succeeded in revealing what our earliest gardens *may* have looked like. We can make a fairly safe assessment of primitive horticultural practices, and assemble similar plants in reasonably accurate reconstructions of early gardens. But among all the various elements of garden design and construction, topiary exists, a sort of horticultural dinosaur, as a clear and well-established living link with the earliest gardens. Since Classical times, and perhaps even earlier, topiary has survived the vagaries of fashion, its popularity waxing and waning. But topiary seems to be so deeply entrenched in the hearts of so many gardeners, that it is unlikely ever to disappear from the garden scene.

It may be that the Egyptians clipped their trees into tidy shapes, but this can be deduced only from their tomb paintings, which, after all, are more symbolic than representational. It is only in the gardens of ancient Rome that we can be certain of finding topiary, and its immediate acceptance by the upper echelons of Roman society as a desirable garden adornment was

Levens Hall, Cumbria

guaranteed, since it was introduced by Cneius Matius, one of Julius Caesar's circle and an even more intimate friend of the Emperor Augustus.

The earliest description of topiary features in a garden is given by the Roman Consul, Pliny the Younger (AD 62–110), writing about his Tuscan garden. Near the house assorted topiary figures were displayed within a box hedge. The descending walk down an easy slope was bordered by topiary animals cut from box, and led to a lawn with a path around its circumference shaded by evergreens clipped into a variety of shapes. Further on there was an area known as the *gestatio*, 'laid out in the form of a Circus, ornamented in the middle with Box, cut into numberless different figures, together with a plantation of shrubs prevented by the shears from running too high: the whole is fenced in by a Wall, covered with Box, rising in different ranges to the top.'

There was a straight walk from which other other paths led into 'rooms' each quite different in character: 'In one place you have a little meadow; in another the Box is cut into a thousand different forms; sometimes into letters expressing the name of the master; sometimes that of the artificer; whilst here and there little Obelisks rise intermixed alternately with fruit trees, when on a sudden you are surprised with an imitation of the negligent beauties of rural Nature, in the centre of which lies a spot surrounded with a knot of dwarf Plane Trees.'

Reading through that account of a Roman garden, I was immediately reminded of certain gardens that I visited in the course of researching this book: Chastleton Manor's 'circus' of topiary figures; the garden rooms at Hidcote Manor and the antique terraced arbour at Rous Lench Court. How these gardens of the late nineteenth and early twentieth centuries came to have such close ties with the gardens of ancient Rome can be discovered in the repeatedly rekindled love affair between the garden designers and architects of England and France with the design heritage of Italy.

Happily, we again appear to be enjoying one of these romances. There is a desire for formality in garden layout, which, coupled with the use of sweet simple flowers, creates an air of tranquillity and security – qualities missing from many high tech, 'Big Bang' lives.

The landscapes of Capability Brown, created during an age of confident expansionism and increasing wealth have little relevance today – not least because there are few people with the acreage or the means to create or maintain a 'garden' on such a broad canvas. Rather, we wish to put a small knot of herbs near the house, beds of roses and perennials either side of a gentle walk that leads to a small carpet of wild flowers beneath the orchard trees. This is the type of garden that can be created on virtually any scale, from a country acre to a city courtyard. It behoves us to look, as our ancestors did, at the gardens of Renaissance Italy, and borrow from these beautiful exemplars. One of the main lessons to learn is the use of hedges and single shrubs, clipped into simple or fantastic shapes, as a device to give focus to a garden scheme or to contain the whole.

After the fall of Rome and during the ensuing 'Dark Ages', gardens turned in on themselves, of necessity; it would have been foolhardy to create a rolling vista of clipped trees and garden rooms terraced down a hillside, up which marauding vandals could conveniently charge. Safe behind the castle curtain wall, the only garden was the *hortus conclusus*, a trellis-fenced enclosure. The brothers in the neighbouring monastery would preserve the plants and gardening skills of a bygone age.

Topiary was no longer the important feature it had once been, although a look at a medieval manuscript illumination, like the flower garden shown in the fifteenth-century Grimani breviary reveals that it was used occasionally. Small rectangular raised beds are planted at the centre with single trees whose foliage has been clipped into 'cakestand' shelves ringing naked narrow trunks. However, a popular form of trained tree during this period was the arbour or 'herber'; the branches of parallel rows of trees (lime for preference) were pruned and plashed to make walls and a roof overhead. Often the branches were trained to allow boards to be run across them in order to create a floor, eight or nine feet above ground and running the length of the arbour. A hint of this can be seen at Levens Hall where the topmost branches of the beech hedge have been trained to take boards on which the gardeners can stand, enabling them to clip the top of the hedge – from the inside, out.

The first great age of English garden design began in the early sixteenth century. The layout of the garden remained medieval, but what altered was the scale of the undertaking, castle walls were falling; the motivation, beautifully executed gardens were an immediate reference to wealth and social standing; and guiding principles, gleaned from translations of the classical texts of Pliny, Democratus and others. In these texts, the Renaissance

English gardener found frequent reference to topiary work. This rediscovered skill was most admirably exercised in the gardens of Hampton Court Palace. Work accounts for the period after the hapless Wolsey passed his palace to Henry VIII, show payment for 'anticke' work, or curiously shaped trees. Later, near the end of Elizabeth I's reign, the writings of a German traveller describe the privy gardens as he saw them in 1599, containing centaurs, servants with baskets, figures of men and women, all wrought in topiary. Evidently, what we see today is but a pale shadow of the garden's former self.

Topiary's popularity really peaked early in the eighteenth century after about twenty years of Dutch influence engendered by the reign of William and Mary. It must be said of Dutch garden design that it had more than a hint of the theme park about it. Land was scarce in Holland, and so the various garden elements had to be rigorously disciplined: little toy bridges crossed doll-sized canals, coloured glass, glittering gold and gaily polychromed ornament took the place of untidy flower beds and elaborate knots, and topiary ruled supreme.

George London and his partner Henry Wise, the most famous nurserymen of the period, were notorious for their devotion to topiary, importing most of their stock from Holland. They deemed bay, pyracantha, *Arbutus unedo*, *Prunus laurocerasus* and species of *Phillyrea* all worthy of topiary treatment. The publication in 1662 of John Evelyn's *Sylva* did much to promote the use of yew for topiary; previously, box had predominated.

It was during this time that the great houses of England, designed by the likes of Vanbrugh and Wren, Castle Howard and the addition to Hampton Court Palace for instance, were being constructed and set in gardens created to relate directly to the scale of the building, with the use of topiary, hedges, arbours, parterres and mazes echoing the 'hard' architectural elements.

Meanwhile, discontented whisperings offstage were getting louder. 'I have not seen any garden in Italy worth taking notice of. The Italians fall as short of the French in this particular, as they excel them in their palaces . . .', wrote Joseph Addison in *Remarks on Several Parts of Italy in the Years 1701, 1702, 1703*. He did withdraw the barb somewhat by continuing, 'it is to the honour of the Italians, that the French took from them the first plans of their gardens, as well as of their waterworks; so that the surpassing of them at present is to be attributed to their riches rather than the excellence of their taste.' This was

Haseley Court, Oxfordshire

followed by Alexander Pope's snide commentary on the trend for the formal in garden design: 'Our trees rise in cones, globes and pyramids. We see the marks of the scissors upon every plant and bush . . . I would rather look upon a tree when in all its luxuriancy and diffusion and branches, than when it is thus cut and trimmed into a mathematical figure'. A year later, in 1713, he continued the offensive with a spurious list 'of greens to be disposed of by an eminent town-gardener' and which included 'St George in box; his arm scarce long enough . . . A green dragon of the same with a tail of ground-ivy for the present . . . An old Maid of Honour in wormwood . . . A topping Ben Johnson in Laurel'.

Popular opinion was swept along on this vitriolic tide. William Kent, his protégé Capability Brown and a host of lesser talents descended on the English formal garden in one of those collective acts of cultural vandalism that is difficult to forgive. Few escaped; Levens Hall is a refugee of the Landscape Movement. One can only imagine the numbers of ancient topiary specimens that were grubbed up and burned, and all that remains now of England's finest gardening hour are crumbling walls and faint outlines in the turf after a severe drought.

The circumvolutions of history are, occasionally, comforting. In this particular instance the anti-landscape movement was born before the century was out. In 1794, Uvedale Price wrote *An Essay on the Picturesque*, condemning Brown and Repton for their barbaric deeds. He wrote: 'I may perhaps have spoken more feelingly on this subject for having done myself what I so condemn in others, destroyed an old fashioned garden . . . I doomed it and all its embellishments, with which I had formed such an early connection to sudden and total destruction . . . I remember, that even this garden (so infinitely inferior to those of Italy) had an air of decoration, and of gaiety, arising from that decoration.' This learned country squire speaking out with such sad eloquence against a popular trend gave focus to what others were no doubt feeling. After seeing Kent's planting of dead trees in Kensington Gardens, 'to give the greater air of truth to the scene', perhaps they even began to wonder if Brown and the others were nothing more than marketplace opportunists, creating a demand where previously none had existed?

The question was raised and the answer was a swing to the 'old-fashioned' garden ideal. This laid the foundation of much that occurred in garden design

Beckley Park, Oxfordshire

during the early part of this century and the end of the last. Italian gardens were once again the model. Formality was achieved with box-edged beds devoted to floricultural wonders, and emblematic parterres of brightly coloured bedding-out were highly desirable. Topiary was making a quiet comeback, helped most notably by the romanticism of the Pre-Raphaelite Brotherhood, and in particular by William Morris who approved of the architectural use of trained trees and shrubs and was keen on topiary features.

The Arts and Crafts Movement was topiary's saviour. Its followers idealised the rural skills of 'olde' England, which included the art of garden-making. Allied to this was their belief that the architect was the only one capable of designing a garden to accompany the house on which he was working. Two influential books published within months of each other in 1891–2 were Reginald Blomfield's *The Formal Garden in England* and J. D. Sedding's *Garden Craft Old and New*.

Blomfield was an architect and a leading authority on Renaissance architecture. His book was one of the first to examine the lost formal gardens of England and advocate a return to that style. It also served as a platform for his condemnation of the landscape style. In conclusion he wrote, 'an attempt has been made in this book to show the essential reasonableness of the principles of Formal Gardening, and the sanity of its method when properly handled. The long yew-hedge is clipped and shorn because we want its firm boundary lines and the plain mass of its colour; the grass bank is formed into a definite slope to attain the beauty of close-shaven turf at varied angles with the light . . . The formal garden lends itself readily to designs of smaller gardens within the garden.'

Sedding was also an architect whose work was much admired by Morris and Burne-Jones. He was a leading member of the Art Worker's Guild and his love of gardening was no doubt generated by his devotion to Renaissance Italian gardens. 'Of the gardens of Italy, who shall dare to speak critically. Child of tradition: heir by unspoken descent, inheritor of the garden-craft of the whole civilised world. It stands on a pinnacle high above the others, peerless and alone: fit for the loveliest of lands . . . splendidly adorned, with straight terraces, marble statues, clipped ilex and box . . . so frankly artistic, yet so subtley blending itself in the natural surroundings . . .'. His book was a highly personal view of the form a garden should take, and is illustrated by watercolour perspectives of his design ideals. Topiary clipped into extravagant geometric shapes is much in evidence, as are box parterres and high hedges dividing the garden into rooms.

The *yang* to the formalists *yin* came in the shape of William Robinson, guru to the new generation of landscape gardeners and whose books *The Wild Garden* and *The English Flower Garden* railed against garish bedding-out in formal design. Of old-fashioned gardens he wrote, 'The planners of [these gardens] prided themselves upon being able to give Nature lessons of good behaviour, to teach her geometry and the fine Art of irreproachable lines; but Nature abhors lines; she is for geometers a reluctant pupil.' To which Sedding replied, 'Mr Robinson . . . humbly skirts his ground with a path which as nearly represents a tortured horse-shoe as Nature would permit; and his trees he puts in a happy-go-lucky way, and allows them to nearly obliterate his path at their own sweet will! No wonder he does not fear Nature's revenge, where is so little Art to destroy!'

In Blomfield's and Sedding's books, Robinson thought he smelled a rat and his wrath was terrible to behold. Sedding's and Blomfield's theories were pilloried in *Garden Design and Architect's Gardens* which Robinson published in 1892. Robinson compared topiary to the binding of Chinese women's feet and avowed that the only forgiveable reason for clipping a tree was for purely practical purposes, never for ornament. Art and function were at war, and the concept of improving nature through art acquired a new following.

Arguments such as these have kept the use of topiary alive, and certainly the gardens of our recent past, which are the ones that we most admire, were the products of compromise between Art and Nature. The importance of form in the garden plan became a precept, and it was accepted that trees clipped in geometric shapes provided this element. Furthermore, when so many contemporary garden designs contain architectural elements, and the cost of hard materials, the sculptures and ornaments, is so prohibitive, we should look at the use of low clipped hedges instead of brick walls, *cabinets de verdure* rather than cedarwood summer-houses on swivel bases, and boxwood peacocks in preference to an antique statue or precast concrete *Mannequin Pis*.

## Chastleton Manor
### *Oxfordshire*

Silent, serene and just a little spooky, the early 17th-century manor house reposes on a hill overlooking the tiny hamlet at its feet. This is one of England's best historic houses and the topiary pleasaunce one of the country's most important garden relics; the box figures are acknowledged as being of great age, dating from the early 18th century. The encircling yew hedges were planted at a much later date. Over the centuries the figures have lost their definition, but a photograph from a 1902 edition of *Country Life* shows the box at two hundred years old. Several figures suggest chessmen – a knight and a pawn, a crown and castle – there is also a basket, and a fanciful finial or two, and the circular lawn in which they stand is seen cut into triangular and curved flower beds marked with standard roses.

The topiary is clipped once a year by a local farmer who has been tending it over the last fifteen years, but as this job coincides with the harvest it is not always possible to clip at exactly the right time. He has also noticed that the box is now becoming more difficult to keep in shape, with the branches becoming looser as the girth of the bushes increases, which makes them more prone to wind and snow damage.

# Brickwall
## *West Sussex*

The gardens in front of this Elizabethan house are an excellent example of how the early English formal garden achieved breathtaking effects within a comparatively small area by a clever manipulation of space, using changes of level and impressive plantings of yew and box constantly to change the scale. The path from the house into the garden leads immediately from the door into a 130-feet-long walk bordered by massive yews. These trees screen the fishpond and parterre on either side from view and the whole is surrounded by a walk raised above the level of the terrace. A double yew hedge separates the remaining garden area, entered through arches which are staggered to prevent a straight path and vista.

The gardens at Brickwall are being restored, and a chessboard has been planted to complement the two hundred and fifty year old yew tetrahedrons. The metal framework will guide the clipping as the yews grow. Any shoots that protrude beyond the frame are trimmed away and when the frame is full, it is removed leaving a perfectly shaped chess piece. To some topiarists the use of a frame was anathema as the practice of the true art meant shapes could only be trimmed by eye. However, such an enormous undertaking as this chessboard is helped by the use of frames, and also turns the area into a sculpture garden long before the topiary has matured.

## Hever Castle
*Kent*

W. W. Astor, the American millionaire who restored Hever Castle at the turn of this century, purchased the topiary for the Anne Boleyn garden from Messrs J. Cheal & Sons of Crawley, Sussex and their rivals in the trade, the unbelievably named firm of Messrs Wm. Cutbush & Son, Highgate, in north London. Herbert Cutbush was most actively engaged in supplying the topiary revivalists and travelled frequently to Boskoop, Holland, 'where examples were being steadily developed, securing options on these and purchasing all that were well advanced.' The enterprising *boomkmeckers* created every manner of animal and bird, geometric shapes, and sundry oddities like tables with chairs, and even churches.

Astor made his garden in 1904, the year Edith Wharton published her book on Italian villa gardens. At Hever the Italian garden is quite separate from the old English garden with its cluster of peacocks and spectacular golden yew chessmen. These were modelled after gaming figures that Astor saw in the British Museum and which dated from the reign of Henry VIII, Hever having been the childhood home of Anne Boleyn and the scene of her seduction of (or by) Henry VIII.

The yew maze at Hever measures 75 feet square and was planted in 1905. Hedge mazes had returned to popularity in the early 1800s, modelled after antique examples such as the maze at Hampton Court Palace, one of the oldest hedge mazes in England, and dating from 1690. The earliest mazes were simple patterns etched in the turf. They were originally part of pagan rituals, later co-opted by Christianity. Contrite sinners were urged to creep about the maze on their knees, asking forgiveness and coming to terms with the idea of the Resurrection. However, the hedge maze was an Elizabethan innovation, and intended purely for fun.

## Hatfield House
*Hertfordshire*

Next to the knot garden at Hatfield, on the other side of a lime tree walk, and below the west front is a herbaceous garden of island beds – but with a difference. Instead of the tired and typical kidney shapes the beds are arranged in a pattern derived from a piece of antique lace, and enclosed within a high protective yew hedge. It is claimed that island beds are a modern innovation, but this part of the garden was laid out ninety years ago. The beds are edged with brick laid on a thin shelf of sand which makes lawn edge trimming easier.

The formal beds in the private garden are edged with box and filled with peonies, deliciously scented shrub roses, sweet peas and other old-fashioned favourites. During the Victorian period the beds formed an intricate paisley pattern planted up with thousands of fuchsias and studded with rose arbours, all tended by a battalion of gardeners. At one time 103 men and boys were employed in the grounds; today there are five, and they keep the gardens immaculate without the aid of chemicals as Lady Salisbury will not permit their use among the flowers. All the box edgings are weeded by hand and excellent horticultural practice combined with the abundant birdlife keeps the insects and other nasties at bay.

The parallel avenues of *Quercus ilex*, holm oak, define the north–south edges of the private garden. The trees were brought from France where they seem to specialise in growing woody plants on legs or stilts. The lollipop heads are clipped once at the end of July which gives the wood time to seal over and ripen before the onset of winter; important for a south European native. At Hatfield the stilts are lagged to protect the trees from winter damage; burlap sacking has given way to bubble plastic as the insulating material, since it is durable and versatile and can be used on tender subjects throughout the garden.

# The Grand Manner

Elizabeth I received news of her accession at Hatfield and the knot garden made in the courtyard of the Old Palace is intended to recall the gardens as she would have known them. Lady Salisbury's design was inspired by the discovery of an early sketch of the garden which showed that in addition to a knot, there was a maze and an orchard. Like her other knot garden at Cranbourne House (see page 82), her ladyship has used 16th- and 17th-century flowers and an abundance of old-fashioned roses, as well as four almond trees, and a quickset hedge which marks the perimeters of the knot. The box plants for the knot pattern were grown from cuttings of the current year's growth taken at the end of summer, 3–4 inches long, with a heel. These were dipped in hormone rooting powder and lined out in a coldframe in an even mix of sharp sand, leaf mould and peat. The plants were lifted and planted out in position the following spring: 11,000 in double rows, 5–6 inches apart.

There are two mazes at Hatfield; a small penitential box maze forming one quarter of the knot garden in front of the Old Palace, and this elaborate yew hedge maze on the bottom terrace of the private gardens below the east front of the mansion. At the centre of the maze two topiary lions rest at the foot of a topiary tree stump. The maze is clipped once at the end of summer and fed in the autumn with nitrate of soda, mulched for the winter and then fed twice during summer with fish, blood and bone. This feeding regime is particularly recommended for newly planted yews; regular feeding can produce up to eighteen inches of growth a year.

# Nymans
*West Sussex*

The walled garden and the topiary enclosure near the burned out shell of the library are the only formal parts of a garden which exists chiefly to provide a home for the collection of rare and unusual plants, assembled by the Messel family who came to Nymans in 1890. At most times of the year this garden is full of flowers from the azaleas, rhododendrons and old shrub roses for which it is famous, and from a multitude of other choice plants. But in early March the uniform shapes, dull texture and deep tints of the topiary provide a striking contrast to the profusion of colour and textures provided by surrounding plantings of shiny leaved *Chosiya ternata* and *Magnolia grandiflora*, the towering spire of *Cryptomeria japonica*, and the explosion of toast-brown azalea seedheads.

The almost circular walled garden, created in 1904, is divided into quarters by two paths marked at their intersection with an Italian fountain, and four grand topiary figures shaped like enormous orbs from outsize regalia. One path is planted with spring bulbs and the other with summer-flowering herbaceous perennials, the planting recommended by William Robinson – his opinion of the topiary is not recorded! The topiary is over seventy years old and shrubs planted nearby had outgrown their space and were beginning to damage the growth of the yews. This is often a problem and the only remedy is to remove the offending overgrowth, cut out the damaged branches of yew and begin a regime of feeding to encourage new growth to break.

# Orchards
*Surrey*

A product of the 'tasteful and ingenious' brain of Edwin Lutyens, the 'Dutch' garden is a series of secluded 'rooms' and passages to other parts of the garden formed by seven feet tall yew hedges. It is laid out below a loggia terrace, the vantage point for enjoying the distant view of the Thorncombe valley. This is Lutyens at his best. He was the master of uniting a house and garden with the landscape, consistently disproving the theory that if there is a view to enjoy, a garden is superfluous: the two will constantly be at odds with each other, fighting for attention. But here the garden is concealed and the view predominant until one descends from the loggia. Then the view is lost and garden takes over.

# Beckley Park
*Oxfordshire*

The manor house dates to around 1550 and is surrounded by three moats, only parts of which remain. It was purchased in 1919 by Percy Feilding. He was an architect and keen on Italian Renaissance gardens, which is not surprising since he had studied under Reginald Blomfield. Three years later he began planting the box and yew to make a formal garden to complement the Tudor building, creating three main areas within the middle and inner moat gardens. The first is a collection of yew topiary figures ranged in two parallel rows enclosed within a yew hedge. No two are the same: wedding cake, spiral, pyramids, a bear and peacock, and sundry other geometric shapes.

Percy Feilding was a great friend of Lady Ottoline Morrell and it is thought that he may have had a hand in the design of the garden at Garsington Manor. Mr Feilding died when his own garden was seven years old, and his son Basil, with the help of a friend, took on the work of shaping the hedges, without altering the original layout. The garden in the inner moat lies immediately before the house, and is given mostly to lawns surrounded by a tall hedge with pyramid crenellations and spheres along its top. Mr Feilding wrote of topiary that it 'enhances the garden design with solid bulk and firm line, [a quality that is] unobtainable with the loose softness of natural growth'.

An arch in the far end of the yew hedge leads into a box knot arranged in quarters and with the box hedges of each bed shaped into four pentagonal segments around a central pyramid. In the mid-1960s, a visit from the American Boxwood Society and identification by the Oxford Botanic Garden revealed that there are at least five varieties of *Buxus sempervirens* in the garden and one of *B. balearica* which has a larger leaf and bluer colouring. When the Society asked how the topiary was fed and mulched, the answer was, 'Nothing, nothing, never, never'; it still is! After the Second World War, some of the hedges were cut back by half to reduce the overgrowth. Today the hedges are trimmed once a year between May and the first frosts at the end of September.

## Haseley Court
*Oxfordshire*

In 1542 the historian John Leland recorded that, 'At Little Haseley master Barentyre hath a right fair mansion place and marvellous fair walkes, *topiarii operis*, and orchards and ponds.' The trees of the present topiary were planted in 1850 and the records of a past owner refer to their being clipped into shapes around 1900. Fifty-five years later when Mrs Lancaster took on the property it was virtually derelict. The house was a shambles thanks to the troops billeted there during the war, and the gardens overgrown. Curiously, the topiary, though choked with weeds, was perfectly clipped thanks to the attentions of an old gentleman who bicycled over each season from Great Haseley to give his 'kings and queens' as he called them, all the attention they deserved.

## Rodmarton Manor
*Gloucestershire*

This is the quintessential Arts and Crafts house and garden, designed by Ernest Barnsley for the Hon. Claud Biddulph, and furnished entirely by the community of artist–craftsmen he established with the Gimson brothers at nearby Sapperton. Barnsley had trained with the architect J. D. Sedding and was associated with Reginald Blomfield; his layout for the garden reflected the ideals of these two men. Peacocks and fanciful finials, and 'other shapes the yew wanted to make' adorn the tall hedges that section the south front terrace into intimate seating areas. Only by walking out of these enclosures to the edge of the terrace can one discover the distant view of the Vale of White Horse. At the same time, the hedges provide a shelter belt for the winter-flowering and tender subjects that clothe the south-facing walls of the house.

The beds of the Long garden are broader than those designed by Barnsley and are part of the extensive restorations carried out by Mrs Biddulph and her late husband since 1954. There is a feeling of spaciousness in this part of the garden, unimpaired by the broad borders, the tall yew hedges which wall it all round, and the yew buttresses that flank the pool at its centre. A slow stroll along the arrow straight path through this Jekyllesque garden ends in a summer house designed by Ernest Barnsley. He believed that a garden was an extension of the house and its divisions equivalent to rooms; this then is the ballroom.

A small enclosure known as the 'Troughery' divides the terrace from the Leisure garden. This part of the garden is given to a collection of topiary cakestands and cannon balls and redundant stone troughs collected from around the estate and pressed into service to house diminutive alpines. The bones of the pleached limes which cloister the chapel corner of the house frame the entrance to this peaceful small corner, while the arrangement of path and topiary leads the eye out of the garden and across the fields.

## Ilmington Manor
### *Warwickshire*

Work on this garden began in 1919. Created by the current owner Mr Flowers' parents; his mother was the keen gardener and his father was the planner, it was made in the remains of an old orchard and surrounding area of rough grass. An album of family photographs shows the garden in 1924, and after only five years the hedges were established and the topiary shapes well-defined; but not only were the shapes much smaller, they were quite different in design. The cakestands with their conical tops began as cylinders topped by three spheres in a traffic light arrangement, and only the bases for the huge shapes in the Dutch garden existed, like hairy green ottomans dotted about a sitting room.

Over the years the topiary had begun to sprawl and become untidy, so it is now clipped tightly each year at summer's end to restore the shapes; those in the Dutch garden were originally peacocks and these are being given new heads. Where the topiary may have started out as an amusing incident seen within a framework of flower borders and specimen trees and shrubs, the clipped shapes and battlemented hedges grew in stature eventually to become the strongest feature in the garden against which all else is measured.

## Great Dixter
*East Sussex*

In 1904, Hermann Muthesius wrote in his book *The English House*, 'Clipped hedges are the walls by means of which the garden designer delimits his areas . . . just as clipped trees, by repetition of the same geometric form, establish certain geometric compositions in the garden. Thus topiary work is one of the principal elements of garden design in general; the indispensable means of establishing form.' Eleven years later, one of the main exponents of 'architectural' garden design, Nathaniel Lloyd, published his book *Garden Craftsmanship in Box and Yew*, as an authoritative guide to making garden enclosures, without which 'the feelings of protection, of peacefulness and of repose are altogether lacking.'

At the time when gardens like Dixter were being made, there was a tremendous influx of plants into England from all corners of the Empire. The creation of small sheltered areas within the garden was useful for protecting tender subjects, and the hedges themselves provided the perfect setting for plant collections, a perfect foil for the myriad colours and shapes of flower and foliage. Today, Nathaniel Lloyd's son, Christopher, is one of England's foremost plantsmen, and while he has no inclination to create topiary, preferring 'making plants' to making shapes, he appreciates topiary and will go out of his way to see it. For him topiary's great attraction is the way its formality complements informal planting in the garden and he believes that that is what gave the old cottage gardens their appeal.

In *The Adventurous Gardener*, Mr Lloyd describes the maintenance of a mature hedge. Fear is the amateur's greatest liability and this is especially evident when it comes to cutting back a hedge that has become overgrown, yew in particular. He advises cutting boldly into the centre of the bush, cutting back much further than the overgrowth appears to warrant. Strong new growth comes back much more evenly from the centre (trunk) than from anywhere near the outside. The base of a hedge must be kept clear of encroaching weeds, ivy especially, and the level of soil around the base renewed as it erodes. Each year in early spring the yew at Dixter is surface fed with fish, blood and bone; a slow acting organic yearly feed recommended for all hedges.

The garden around the old manor house of Dixter was Nathaniel Lloyd's proving ground, and anyone who has visited this greatest of English gardens will understand immediately what he and Muthesius meant, and also what gives 'the English Garden' its distinctive character: the house, by its close integration with the surrounding garden through the use of hedged enclosures, transmits its intimacy to the garden. The Lloyds came to the property in 1910 and engaged Edwin Lutyens to make alterations to the house and to design the gardens. With the house at the centre, and the various areas of the garden set out around it, most areas are immediately accessible, 'a satisfyingly intimate arrangement' is how Christopher Lloyd describes it in his book *The Year at Great Dixter*.

In his garden chronicle, Mr Lloyd describes how in October the showpiece is the old Lavender Garden with its array of eighteen yew peacocks united by a double hedge of purple-hued *Aster lateriflorus* 'Horizontalis', and in December that he enjoys 'the clean lines of winter . . . The yew hedges and topiary look smart, especially on a frosty morning when their tops are white.' The clearly defined shapes of topiary and clipped hedge contribute so much to making a garden more interesting during winter, particularly as they throw into sharp focus the colours and shapes which are there in leaf and branch.

## Levens Hall
*Cumbria*

Walking into the garden at Levens Hall is one of the most heart-stopping moments a visitor to topiary collections is likely to experience. It is difficult to imagine the extraordinary variety of shapes. The jungle-like effect of all those shades of emerald green, lemon yellow and eau-de-nil blue from the yew and box makes the place look like the Emerald City of Oz. But most outstanding is the sheer size of the topiary for which nothing can prepare you. Levens is the oldest topiary garden in England – a true gardening time capsule. The original plan was determined by Monsieur Beaumont, who came to Levens in 1689, the year his previous master, James II abdicated. It is said Beaumont was a pupil of Le Nôtre, and the garden reflects that influence. But it has none of the theatrical grandeur of Le Nôtre and is decidedly more entertaining to stroll through – more 'user-friendly'.

Guillaume Beaumont was engaged by Colonel James Grahme to lay out the grounds around his Tudor manor house. From 1690 to 1720 they worked at creating a garden that was later described by William Gilpin as 'all that is best in Landscape and Design'. The gardens were world renowned and people made the then tortuous journey from London especially to view the gardens. Levens survived probably because it has remained within the same family since its creation, its fame and notoriety forming a sizeable part of their legacy. There is a map of the garden *c*.1745 showing the main avenues of beech hedge dividing the grounds into quarters beyond the topiary parterres near the house. More than two centuries later, the layout is unchanged, making Levens the finest example of a gentleman's garden, pre-Landscape Movement.

The topiary is never fed as each year the flower beds are mulched with farmyard manure. One or two pieces have been cut hard back to restore growth; Mr Crowther, the head gardener, recommends feeding trees well during the year prior to pruning to build up their strength. In many gardens *Tropaeolum speciosum*, the Flame Flower, has been trained over, or rather into, the old yews. The vivid scarlet blossoms, like mini-nasturtiums (to which family it belongs) look spectacular against the inky green yew. At Levens there are quantities of the vine, and Mr Crowther cautions against letting it ramp away too freely. They have found it can cause damage since it eventually forms thick sheets which prevent light and air from reaching the leaves of the yew, thereby killing out large sections of the tree.

One of the quarters made by the beech avenues at Levens Hall in Cumbria holds the bowling green where a lavish entertainment held by Grahme led to the institution of an annual 'Radish Feast'. Each 12 May, the Mayor and Corporation of Kendal would convene in state with numerous other guests to consume wheelbarrows full of radishes, eaten with brown bread and butter, and all washed down with Morocco. Toasts were drunk – 'Luck to Levens while the Kent flows' – ending in such bad behaviour that the feasts were eventually suspended. In around 1900, a gardener clipping one of the oldest yews found a 'Toby Jug' actually embedded in the bark at the top of the main trunk – probably put there by a drunken joker.

Clipping begins in August with the beech hedges and is complete by mid-September when work begins on the topiary and box edgings. This is usually complete by Christmas. All clipping is done by eye as the great age of the topiary means the shapes are quite tight, so it is relatively easy to clip off new growth accurately with small electric shears. Nevertheless, the geometric shapes are still tricky. It is thought that some of the older pieces, especially those 'on stilts' may have been as much as ten feet tall when they were planted. The box topiary and edging are clipped by hand since they are smaller and must be done more slowly. So far, the late clipping and cold northern winters haven't damaged the freshly clipped box.

All the pieces have identities: Queen Elizabeth and her Maids of Honour; jugs of 'Morocco' – the potent brew that was a Levens speciality; Dutch Oven; Judge's Wig; Bellingham Lion – a family crest; Wigwam; Umbrella, as well as the expected chess pieces, bells, spirals and pyramids that are part of the topiary vernacular. In the early 19th century new topiary was added in the old kitchen garden in front of the gardener's cottage; the golden yew and the box topiary pieces were innovations of that period. In the early 1900s the box-edged beds around the topiary held herbaceous perennials and the garden had a more cottagey feel. Today they hold formal bedding – 15,000 plants are raised for this purpose – which practice may have been introduced just after the Second World War when the box edging was renewed.

# Elvaston Castle
*Derbyshire*

William Robinson described Derbyshire as being the English county 'most notorious for examples of disfigured trees', and Elvaston as being littered with topiary work, because the landscape gardeners could think of nothing else to do to make the unyieldingly flat grounds interesting. Made between 1830 and 1850, by the 4th Earl of Harrington and his head gardener, William Barron, Elvaston is one of the earliest examples of an instant garden. Many of the topiary pieces, which form the heart of the garden, were fully grown when transplanted to Elvaston. This was the usual practice in those pre-container days, and in the topiary nurseries of the period, trees were systematically moved from one part of the ground to another and their roots dug round annually to prepare them for eventual lifting. Today, Elvaston is a country park, and in the 16th-century-inspired topiary garden, gargantuan peacocks loom over the naughty boys who have turned the box parterre into a BMX track.

# Wightwick Manor
*Wolverhampton*

'Light and shade by turns, but love always', is the inscription on the sundial at the end of the yew walk. The associations of Wightwick are exclusively pre-Raphaelite and both house and garden breathe the rarefied romantic air of that period. The house, dating from 1887, was furnished by William Morris and Co. and the gardens were laid out by the flower painter, Alfred Parsons, RA, with later additions in 1910 of the flagged terrace and oak balustrade, by Thomas Mawson, the most successful garden designer of the Arts and Crafts period. Parsons used green and golden yew to create formal areas of topiary within a hedged enclosure and walks lined with clipped golden holly. Below Mawson's terrace, yew buttresses divide a border into four sections devoted to flowers that grew in William Morris's garden and in Tennyson's garden, as well as in Shelley's and Kempe's.

# Arley Hall
*Cheshire*

Between 1840 and 1860 Rowland and Mary Egerton-Warburton created the garden at Arley. Today it remains largely unchanged, although five generations of the family, two World Wars and the changing economic scene have each left their mark. Perhaps the effects of the last are most noticeable; in 1960, the topiary garden, which lay before the small Tea House, was uprooted since it, as well as the other topiary and formal hedges, were clipped by hand and made three months work for two men, at a time when there were only two men to tend the entire garden. However, the most important 'structural' topiary was retained and this is most notable in the herbaceous border. Planted in 1846, it is one of the earliest examples of this type of gardening. Originally it was two long beds separated by a broad gravel path. The clipped yew buttresses were added in the early 1870s to divide the borders into four sections, and provide interest when the flowers had faded.

Leaving the herbaceous garden one passes through the rose garden, fragrant with the perfume of countless species and shrub roses that were used to replace the topiary garden, into the ilex avenue. Huge holm oak cylinders frame a view to the park. Originally clipped as moderately-sized pyramids, they outgrew their shapes during the First World War. When, after the war, restoration work on the garden began, it was decided that the hard clipping necessary to reclaim the original shapes would be too drastic, and the best that could be done was to make the enormous cylinders we see now. These are clipped each spring, the gardeners working from wheeled scaffolding platforms. During the Second World War many of the yew hedges had also grown into trees, and in the last fifteen years have been restored by cutting side growth back to the trunk and topping them to about five feet, followed by heavy applications of farmyard manure, bonemeal and general purpose fertilisers.

The western approach to Arley Hall is down a long avenue of pleached lime trees, terminating at a gateway surmounted by the Clock Tower. Limes are most popular for this purpose as they are fast growing; the species most often encountered is *Tilia platyphyllos*, but *T.x. euchlora* is also suitable and doesn't attract the plagues of aphids which so often disfigure limes and all that lies beneath them. Pleached trees like this are usually trained against bamboo canes lashed together to form long horizontal supports arranged in parallel rows, two feet apart, and raised from the main tree stake by extending rods of bamboo. As they grow, the lateral branches are tied to the horizontal canes and the uppermost or leading branches are cut away when the desired height is reached. Eventually, the lateral branches can be lashed together and the frame removed.

## Biddulph Grange
*Cheshire*

This garden has been saved from dereliction by a devoted group of people, bewitched by its Victorian exuberance and eccentricity. In 1842 the wealthy industrialist James Bateman set about creating a highly individual and diverse garden in fifteen acres of moorland fringe. Walks leading down from the Italianate mansion past grassy terraces, flanked by formal yew hedges and past a small lake, take the visitor into, literally, another country. Passing through 'China', one eventually reaches 'Egypt'. This bizarre structure of yew has been trained and clipped to resemble Bateman's idea of an Egyptian temple. Biddulph surprises, and to some degree, shocks the eye of the beholder and, like topiary itself, you either love it or hate it. Bateman was the brother-in-law of Roland Egerton-Warburton who made Arley Hall and whose great-granddaughter is Viscountess Ashbrook. Her opinion of Biddulph is, as she readily admits, likely to be construed as heresy. 'It is an example of knowledge without taste'. She believes that the two brothers-in-law were in competition with each other when making their gardens.

## Packwood House
*Warwickshire*

The fact that the garden of Packwood is one of the best surviving examples of 16th- and 17th-century garden layout, complete with mount, gazebos and terrace, is overshadowed by the time-honoured tradition that the towering yew topiary is an ancient representation of the Sermon on the Mount, with Christ and the four Evangelists overlooking the twelve Apostles and the multitude. However, this legend was first recounted by Reginald Blomfield in 1892, who had it from a gardener he met while visiting the garden, and it is possible that Blomfield suspected his leg was being pulled. The avenue of yews known as the Apostles was there during the 1750s, and the remaining topiary was planted during restorations carried out in the 1850s when a new orchard was planted and many of the yews put in as small topiary specimens.

In England yew grows naturally in areas of free-draining chalk. At Packwood the topiary is planted on heavy clay, and in the mid 1970s some of the trees began to die off, particularly those along the main avenue where most of the visiting public walks. The constant traffic was compacting the already heavy soil and the roots were becoming water-logged in spite of being heavily drained. During periods of wet weather the topiary garden had to be closed, and although this is no longer the case, more drainage is being added. The yews are fed once a year with Vitax-Q-4 and the lawns surrounding them with Growmore twice a year, from which the yews also benefit. Clipping takes three months beginning at the end of July; two men work together, one doing the bottom half and the other doing the top half, working from an hydraulic platform.

# Rous Lench Court
*Worcestershire*

Miles Hadfield's description of this garden as, 'one of the finest pieces of topiary in England, massive in design and quite devoid of eccentricity' leaves the visitor unprepared for what is to be found; little seems to have been written about it over the past ninety years, although there are passing references in Pevsner and in Jekyll's *Garden Ornament*, and *Elysian Gardens*, a plea for garden preservation published by Save Britain's Heritage. The seven acre garden, created around the remains of a Restoration design, contains a series of rooms enclosed in yew topiary hedges, with areas of formal lawn linked by grand stone staircases. The garden climbs a west-facing slope in a series of terraces behind the old house, the one directly behind the house being a yew arbour reputedly planted in the late 15th century. For this alone the garden is highly valuable. But the garden's future is uncertain and its continued existence subsequently under threat.

In 1899, at the height of the Robinson, Blomfield and Sedding debate, *Country Life* magazine declared that Rous Lench Court was one of the few properties in the land that retained gardens in keeping with the 'ancient state' of the dwelling: 'It has scarcely a peer in England'. Rous Lench Court is the epitome of the Italianate garden as seen through English eyes. Its improver, the Rev. Chafy-Chafy, came to the property in 1876 and began enlarging and developing the gardens, adding the fountains on the lower of the ten terraces, flower borders and rose gardens and a pinetum. He travelled to Italy and saw how their gardens, made on the hillsides behind the villas, were a progression of separate areas united in most cases by the use of water.

Chafy translated the waterfalls and pools into yew. Two parallel avenues climb the hillsides. One, running up the slope from the ancient arbour roughly through the centre of the garden, is a succession of yew tunnels. The other runs along the roadside boundary of the property and is flanked by vast yew hedges punctuated with arches giving access to the rooms beyond. The topmost terrace is devoted to the walled kitchen garden, divided into quarters bordered with the remains of espaliered fruit trees. The kitchen garden is dominated by a tower, modelled perhaps after the *Palazzo Vecchio* in Florence, providing a bird's eye view of the garden and the Clent hills in the distance.

The terrace below the kitchen garden is bisected by a tunnel and bower, and the terrace below that has at its centre a *cabinet de verdure*, a circular 'summer-house' made from a dozen yew trees, of which six remain. Such features were a popular 16th-century conceit and usually made from pollarded trees: in 1563, Bernard de Pallissy described how to create *cabinets*, and advocated their use in place of 'dragons, cocks, soldiers on horseback and other absurdities cut out of rosemary and other plants.' There are no 'absurdities' at Rous Lench, other than that such a unique garden should be facing extinction, in spite of the efforts of the elderly head gardener who has inherited the house and the one man employed to help him.

Other Victorian and Edwardian topiary gardens relied heavily on 'absurdities' for their impact. The yews at Clipsham Hall in Lincolnshire form a collection of 150 trees clipped into a wild variety of shapes, some of which are embellished with bas-relief camels, elephants and initials. Clipsham garden is contemporary with Rous Lench, but the latter, with its purely architectural use of yew to give structure to the garden, is probably more relevant to our understanding of the development of the English garden.

## Blickling Hall
### *Norfolk*

Few of the houses owned by the National Trust make such an hypnotic first impression as Blickling; the perfect Jacobean mansion sits formal and serene within a frame of majestic yew hedges. Planted at the same time as the house was built in the early 17th century, the hedges are 310 feet long, 17 feet tall and at least 14 feet wide. They are shaped to match the gable ends of the outbuildings flanking the main house. Two gardeners clip the hedges beginning at the end of August, and with the topiary in the formal gardens behind the house, the whole process takes approximately six weeks. During winter it was the usual practice to knock away any snow that settled on the hedges, but this was found to cause just as much damage as leaving it.

The formal gardens behind the house are an adaptation of the flower garden laid out in 1872 by W. A. Nesfield for the Marchioness of Lothian. It was a clutter of small beds filled with tender bedding dotted with rose pergolas and topiary. This included the odd configurations, dubbed the 'grand pianos', at the foot of the steps which lead up to a sweep of lawn, which was just as cluttered, and to the distant Temple. In 1935 Norah Lindsay was brought in to make sense of it all, which she did by creating four blocks of herbaceous planting, unified by the topiary at the corners of each bed. The rest was banished, making a garden that for most of the year is elegantly simple, until the summer when the full-blown herbaceous borders inject a note of informality, frothing like petticoats at the feet of the yews.

## Hidcote Manor
*Gloucestershire*

In 1907 work began on a garden that is now recognised as the paragon of the English garden style. That garden is Hidcote Manor in Gloucestershire and its creator was Major Lawrence Johnston, an American national by birth, but a British citizen by choice. He was a product of that generation of independently wealthy Americans who flocked to Europe at the turn of the last century, avid for the culture and kudos of its society. In exchange, these pioneers to the Old World brought their dollars and their enthusiasm, injecting fresh blood into ageing veins. Johnston's treatment of his garden is symbolic of this exchange; its layout is derivative and planned in the best Arts and Crafts tradition of garden rooms set out within clipped hedges and accented by topiary, but the planting within the rooms was innovative. Johnston was one of the first to shuffle all sorts of plants together, to create what we now practise as mixed planting.

Hidcote Manor is situated on a plateau and the gardens are made around two main axes which lie at a right angle; their point of intersection is on the high ground and marked by twin gazebos. From this vantage point the pleached hornbeams of the Stilt Garden and the Holm oaks either side of the formal gate frame the westerly vista. Two small box-edged beds at the far end contain the only flowers in this section, so the view has little competition. Johnston was born in France and spent the first years of his life there and this arrangement of hornbeams, like a rectangular box and known as *palissades à l'Italienne*, is widely used in France, providing shady spots for games of *boules* on many village squares.

Below the southern side of the Stilt garden is an area known as the Pillar garden for the enormous sugar loaf-shaped yews which punctuate the borders along the walks in this part of the garden. At the height of the season the borders are a mass of peonies, lavender, agapanthus, roses and fuchsia spilling out from between the yews and spreading at their feet. The effect is similar to that achieved by Norah Lindsay, Johnston's closest friend, at Blickling Hall (see page 66).

Hidcote is very similar to the small villa gardens of Tuscany in that each area of the garden is a distinct contrast to its neighbour, but given cohesion by the repeated and architectural use of clipped hedges and mixed topiary shapes. In Italy the contrast is primarily one of light and dark, sun and shade. In England the climate is kinder to plant life and so allows more play. Johnston exploited this so that as well as having the contrasts of broad open vistas and small enclosed areas, like the theatre lawn which is defined by clipped mixed hedges and the intimate cottagey White Garden with its low box hedges and peacocks, the plants used provide ample contrasts of colour and form.

In early spring the box-edged beds of the fuchsia garden are carpeted with *Scilla sibirica*. This diminutive parterre is entered through one of Johnston's famous 'tapestry hedges'; a mix of variegated and green holly, copper beech, box and yew. From here the path leads past two sentinel peacocks into the Bathing Pool garden and then into a small rondel of plain lawn where the circle of grass echoes the circle of water in the previous area. This marks the outer limits of the formal garden, and from this plain ungarlanded area one enters 'Westonbirt', where trees chosen for autumn colour are planted in an informal woodland setting.

The entrance to the Old Rose Walk made on the site of the former kitchen gardens was originally marked by six standard bay trees, but these weren't hardy and the National Trust has replaced them with Portugal laurels. Small standard trees clipped into this umbrella shape are a familiar sight in Italian gardens, particularly in Tuscany, where topiary retains its popularity.

# 2

# TEAPOTS AND PEACOCKS

If the fashion for topiary was promoted by the gentry when creating their elegant gardens, during the years when it was out of favour, the actual practical skills and shapes were preserved in cottagers' gardens. They could not afford to follow the dictates of style, and were even less inclined to do so being broadly conservative, comfortable with the familiar, and the custodians of traditional values. The authentic cottage garden although originally a food producing area became in time a place of beauty as the prosperity of small land-owners improved. They saw what was going on in the manor house garden, liked it, and copied the trends. Parterres were translated into box-edged flower and vegetable beds, a flock of yew peacocks on estate lawns became a broody hen by the cottage door, and territorial rights were claimed by creating a castellated wall from the little privet hedge around the garden.

It has been suggested by Cecil Stewart, in his book *Topiary*, that the peacock shaped bush was introduced by returning Crusaders (they appear to have introduced as many things as the Romans) as a sort of poor man's aviary; an attempt to emulate the fabulous trappings of Byzantium where rare birds and peacocks were displayed as symbols of great wealth. But really the origins of shapes can only be speculation; perhaps the teapot shape became popular when the mania for tea-drinking developed; its introduction and the vogue for topiary work took hold in Holland at roughly the same time.

Apart from peacocks, teapots, cakestands, spirals and crowns, which are just a few of the traditional topiary shapes, each new generation of 'topiartists' makes its own impression so that steam engines, teddy bears, ocean liners and other modern images have been added to the list. Since we seem to be on the threshold of another revival it makes one wonder which

Swannington Manor, Norfolk

contemporary icons will be rendered in 'vegetable sculpture'. Concorde? The Voyager Space Shuttle? Snoopy?

Yew, box, holly and privet are, in order of preference, the most common shrubs used to create topiary, and as mentioned earlier, box was dominant until the late seventeenth century when yew was more widely adopted. Common box, *Buxus sempervirens* is native to Mediterranean countries and has been grown in Britain for such a long time that some people think it might be native. Box Hill, Surrey, and Boxley, Kent both derive their names from the plant. It was an early introduction to North America, and is enormously popular there as a specimen shrub, and a wide range of cultivars are valued as landscaping plants. *B. sempervirens* 'Suffruticosa' is the cultivar used for dwarf edging, but 'Morris Midget' and 'Pincushion' are also good. The last is a form of the hardiest box (*B. microphylla* var. *koreana*) and the leaves take on a nice bronzy sheen in winter.

Box deserves its popularity; it will grow in any soil although it resents wet at the roots. Left to grow its own way box makes an eye-catching shrub, but it doesn't mind being clipped year in year out into fastidiously neat shapes. The scent is not to everyone's liking; Queen Anne loathed it so that she had all the box at Hampton Court grubbed up. But on a humid summer evening, it is to me one of the fragrances most redolent of English gardens.

Yew has the reputation for slow growth, but box is even slower! This is why it is always used for low hedges and border edging. Box prefers an acid soil but will grow in slightly alkaline conditions. Propagation from clippings is rewardingly simple; treat as you would any soft or semi-hard wood cutting. The dwarf variety is difficult and consequently expensive to obtain, but the common variety can be clipped to make a low edging although it will not be so petite. Other small shrubs such as *Teucrium chamaedrys* or winter savory can be used to good effect, but nothing beats a well-grown box edging.

Box usually only needs clipping once in early summer (June in England). Occasionally, in cooler regions, there may even then be a danger of frost in which case clipping should be postponed since box will collapse if frost gets into the wounds. If the summer is particularly wet, the box will probably require a second clip at the end of summer.

Yew is supposedly slow-growing and that is why nowadays people resist planting it; our age is more transient than any before and we are reluctant to plant for the future. However, in one Worcestershire garden I saw a six foot yew hedge, started from seed ten years ago. Having just planted my own hedge with two-foot tall babies I found that sight encouraging. All of the head gardeners I spoke to agreed that once a yew has settled in, it can make up to eight inches or more of growth a year. Obviously, if you want an 'instant' screen, yew is not your plant, but if the hedge is to make a feature or even major contribution to the garden scene, it is the plant to choose. Without doubt, the dense rich green makes a perfect foil for flowering plants. The golden yew is ideal for feature work; the terrace lawns at Shugborough Hall in Leicestershire are planted with cones of golden yew and outlined with lavender.

In 1903, Robert Southey wrote in a letter to G. C. Bedford of his great affinity for ancient buildings, '. . . not absolute ruins, but in a state of decline. Even the clipt yews interest me: and if I found one in any garden that should be mine, in the shape of a peacock, I should be as proud to keep his tail well spread as the man who first carved him.' If only more people had felt that way in the past, we might be better off in examples of antique topiary.

Within the last twenty-five years countless topiary pieces have followed the Edwardian fireplace on to the builder's skip, or fallen prey to a new owner's whim of low maintenance gardening. It is understandable on a large estate where the garden team is reduced from ten pairs of hands to two. But surely one person can deal effectively with a single peacock. The exorbitant price of fashion really is unforgiveable.

There are of course other forces at play, and personal taste is one about which little can be done; the destruction of Compton Wynyates stands out as an example of breathtaking vandalism. Equally unavoidable are the Acts of God, like rogue twenty-ton lorries decapitating the twenty foot peacock on a pedestal at Basing, or an especially hard winter ravaging a similar example at Ashperton (the famous horse and jockey is also gone from that village – another victim of the weather).

However, if you are of Mr Southey's sentiment, and have acquired a piece of yew topiary and wish to preserve it, there are several cardinal rules. First of all, do not be afraid of the yew, the older it is the tougher it gets and if a part has died out or become overgrown you really can cut it right back to the trunk and start again. Use a pruning saw or knife and cut out the unwanted part.

Give the plant the best possible aftercare – a good rich manure mulch, some fish, blood and bonemeal and plenty of water if the climate is dry – and it will recover – slowly, just as an elderly person takes longer to recuperate than a youngster. New growth will shoot from the trunk, and as it grows remove the weakest growths and tie in the strongest branches using tarred string.

Clip yew once a year when it has finished making new growth but not yet gone hard. This is usually near the end of summer to early autumn (late July to mid-September in England). Take off all the new growth, unless you wish to increase the size of the topiary in which case leave about one and a half to two inches.

Yew will grow in any soil but prefers one which is well-drained and alkaline. One of the reasons yew topiary hedges do so well as backgrounds to herbaceous borders is that they adore the annual manure mulch. Of course many yew specimens never receive a scrap of fertiliser and still thrive, but even a biennial feed of a general purpose fertiliser like Growmore, applied after clipping and again in the spring, will be gratefully received. Yew can be propagated from the semi-hard clippings, although not as easily as box. Line them out in a coldframe and cover closely with a polythene sheet to conserve moisture.

Holly is the true snail in the growth race, but makes such an impact as a topiary specimen that it's worth finding the patience to persevere. The 'four fat men' at the corners of Rosemary Verey's knot garden and the cakestand she is cultivating are terrific examples of holly topiary at its best. John Evelyn had a superb holly hedge at Sayes Court, destroyed, much to his chagrin, by his house guest Peter the Great whose idea of fun was to be pushed in a wheelbarrow at great speed in and out of the hedge. There are many forms and species of holly, with variegations gold and silver, the broad leaves crinkly, flat, porcupine-like or smooth-edged. Most of these can be increased from semi-hard cuttings taken in early autumn or late summer. To get the Christmassy berries you need male and female plants.

Any soil is suitable for holly except poorly drained, and it especially likes loose acid soil. Prune as for box. Rabbits love holly and especially in hard winters young trees should, as I now know from bitter experience, be protected (as should nearly everything else in the garden!).

*Fagus sylvatica*, the common beech, its purple-leaved form, and *Carpinus*

Oxley, Wolverhampton

*betulus*, the common hornbeam are all extremely popular for hedging and pleaching to make tunnels, palisades and hedges on stilts, such as the example at Hidcote Manor. But the fan-like habit of their leafy branches makes them unsuitable for topiary work.

Beech keeps its leaves during winter; they dry to a wonderful caramel brown and a hedge of this plant makes a good contribution to the seasonal scene, particularly if yew and box topiary are displayed against it. In summer the young growth of purple beech is a rosy pink. This can be enjoyed for a few days, but then must of course be clipped off to keep the hedge in shape.

'Ugly, useless, short-lived weed', is how the viper-tongued Mr Robinson described privet. *Ligustrum ovalifolium* and its golden variegated form, 'Aureum' are the old work horses amongst hedging plants. It's everywhere, and is so bereft of virtues that it is difficult to understand why. Nothing else will grow well near privet, since it takes all the available nourishment from the soil, the flowers are overpowering in number and odour, and it is only semi-evergreen which can make for some highly abstract topiary.

Readymade box topiary is becoming more readily available, but at a blood-curdling price. That available on the English market is imported from Holland. The Dutch nurseryman I spoke to, who has specialised in wholesale topiary for the past forty years, expressed utter dismay at the 100% mark-up most garden centres slap on: 'and then they wonder why they are left with six out of ten bushes after a year!' For the Dutch market, he can't grow them fast enough, so here are a professional's tips on DIY.

The young plants are potted up and kept indoors during the winter; in the spring they are put outside. When the bushes are about two and a half feet tall and two feet wide, they are planted out and training begins, clipping and tying in at the end of June. The trees are fed with farmyard manure or, more recently, guano from Peru. This is especially good on wet soil and gives the foliage a good deep green. By the time he sells the topiary, carefully lifted and potted up, a bush may be anywhere from six to ten years old.

When planting a hedge or shrub for topiary, dig a trench or hole at least two feet deep. If you can begin preparations a year in advance, then the turves which are taken up can be put aside to rot down and then placed in the bottom of the planting hole. If this isn't possible, put a good one foot layer of well-rotted manure in the bottom of the hole then cover this with topsoil knocked from the turves. Place the trees in the hole with the roots well spread out and backfill, having first mixed a handful or two of bonemeal into the soil. Planting should be done during the dormant season (November to March), and the shrubs be kept well watered during summer; a manure or grass-clipping mulch helps to conserve moisture. Keep a two-feet-wide, grass-free zone around the plants.

It will be several years before the young tree reaches a size suitable to begin clipping into a shape, but it helps to have an idea of what you wish to do. Round shapes are easiest, pyramids and spirals difficult. If your piece will have a base, then work on this can begin while a tuft of leading branches in the centre is allowed to grow to become a chicken, crown, peacock or whatever you settle on. However, most people seem to let the tree suggest what shape to clip.

Use tarred string to tie branches either to each other or to a frame; wire cuts into the flesh as the tree grows, string eventually rots. Be patient, clip carefully – one head gardener's advice was to 'take less than you need, 'cause you can always clip away a bit more, but you can't glue a branch back on'.

## Cranbourne Manor
*Dorset*

The herb garden grows within walls of mellow brick and high clipped yew hedge. In early spring, before the lushness of the planting takes over the garden is given form by the edgings of silvery santolina and ring of standard honeysuckles around the sundial. Shrubby santolina and artemisia, one of the other grey-leaved herbs, are favourite plants for bed-edging. They are easily propagated from springtime clippings; trim the stems below a leaf node and put in pots of loose compost or else line them out in a nursery bed; they grow without fail. The edgings are clipped twice to keep them neat; once when the flowerheads begin to form and again at the end of summer.

John Tradescant the Elder had a hand in creating the original gardens at Cranbourne; he was gardener to King James I and Robert Cecil, and Tradescant's 'bill of charges on being sent to plant trees there', remains in the Cecil family archive. This connection caused Lady Salisbury to plan and plant according to 17th-century principles and the result is an inspiring evocation of an English Renaissance garden.

A range of clipped yew cylinders provides a backdrop to a low mount opposite the knot garden. The mount was an essential feature in a Renaissance garden for this artificial hill provided another vantage point from which to view the patterns of parterres and knots. Throughout the garden survivors of the earlier design, such as the mount and yew hedges, are enhanced by more recent additions, like the topiary sugar loaves lining the walk along the knot garden and the box spiral at its centre.

The knot garden, set against the warm red of the Elizabethan brick wall, is a quartered pattern of clipped box planted with only those flowers which were grown in the 16th and 17th centuries. There are double primroses, gold-laced polyanthus, and spicy scented pinks grow with hyacinths, tulips, tiny snake's head fritillaries and regal Crown Imperials.

# Hole Park
*Kent*

When Mr Barham's grandfather came to Hole Park in 1911 the grounds were thickly planted with laurels, large trees and acres of lawn. Seven years later he started planting the yew hedges and goblets in the parkland in front of the house, and also began chronicling the development of the garden. Thanks to this journal we know that the yews which back the herbaceous borders were planted with two feet deep concrete walls under the soil to keep the roots out of the borders. Perhaps he felt this was necessary because his borders were devoted to dahlias, planted in their hundreds, carefully graded by height and colour. Roots from the yews tangled among the tubers would have made planting and lifting for storage an even more tiresome task than it undoubtedly was.

The sunken garden separates the two lengths of herbaceous border designed by Christopher Lloyd of nearby Great Dixter (see page 42), one length is pink and mauve and the other yellow and white. The dome shapes are part of an arbour behind the hedge. The central dome has its bottom branches trained out to form a skirt supported now by a metal frame, marked at each corner with individual domes. The configuration of these five trees resembles the lime tree arbour which grew during the 17th century at Kleef in the Netherlands. In that confection, the central tree was trimmed into a cakestand with half a dozen or more smaller cakestands piercing its lower tier.

The north border is no longer planted with flowers but the substantial topiary hedge remains. It is enormously wide and is clipped from a plank straddling the width and supported at each end by builder's scaffolding. At one end a *clairvoyée* reveals the beautiful vista of the countryside of Kent – the garden of England. The height of several other hedges in the garden has been lowered to make the most of the beautiful setting. This problem was encountered in several other gardens, and in one the hedge was given a natural concave curve by following the droop of a length of string tied between two stakes positioned at each end of the hedge.

## Athelhampton
### *Dorset*

In 1890, the architect F. Inigo Thomas was asked to salvage a 14th-century hall with Tudor additions and also to create a garden, as no trace of the original remained. Thomas illustrated *The Formal Garden in England*, by Reginald Blomfield, and the gardens as we see them today, with perfectly clipped yew pyramids and hedges, typify the early 20th-century return to formal style. This was just the sort of activity which William Robinson condemned – to make a formal garden was questionable, to have it designed by an architect, unforgiveable.

## Rangeworthy
*Avon*

Forty-five feet long and nine feet wide, an 0–6–0 shunting engine keeps company with a Venetian gondola. Both are fashioned from a privet hedge and were started over twenty years ago, when Mr Adrian Powell took over the garden. He uses electric shears to clip his masterpieces, usually at least four times from spring to late autumn, more if summer rains are heavy causing the bushes to grow twice as quickly. But these pieces are just a part of a much larger collection. As with all hobbies, the making of topiary finally became an obsession. A walk through the two and three-quarter acre garden reveals a horse-drawn sleigh hauling beer barrels, a sentry on duty, a baby dinosaur and two overstuffed armchairs for the boxwood crinoline lady and gentleman to relax in after walking the dog. Topiarists never give up, there is always another hedge to make something of, and Mr Powell's golden leylandii are slowly becoming a Cotswolds village, complete with church.

## Reddish House
*Wiltshire*

The home of the late Sir Cecil Beaton is set within a yew hedge of great age where the topiary has long since lost its figure. This is inevitable since even the closest clipping will still leave a scrap of new growth, and over a century later the original design will hardly be discernible. Very few gardens seem to have a record of the original topiary but a careful study of the way branches are growing can given an indication of former shapes.

## Nr Horsham
*Sussex*

All that remains of a cottage and its garden is this lonely yew peacock, hard by a busy road connecting the two market towns of Guildford and Horsham. Beautifully manicured, a diamond in the rough – even the people in the nearby house were unaware of his existence, and it's a good eight feet tall – yet someone comes out annually to clip him over.

## Rudgwick
*Surrey*

A photograph taken in 1900 shows that at one time this 15th-century cottage was three separate dwellings and the topiary wedding cake a spiral of six twists, although it was roughly the same height, ten feet. The rest of the garden contained a few fruit trees and cabbages and it is easy to speculate that the yew is of as great an age as the cottage, since it was the tradition to plant a single tree by the entrance or chimney to protect the house from evil winds and spirits.

# Shalford
*Surrey*

This late 16th-century cottage was once the home of Ambrose Gordon Forsyth who in the 1950s was a garden journalist working for *Popular Gardening* and *The Daily Telegraph*. Born in 1902, he doubtless cut his horticultural teeth on the gardens of Lutyens and Jekyll, so that when he designed his own garden he planted the low box hedge punctuated with cushions in the best tradition of cottage garden vernacular. The bays formed by the cushions make neat planting areas to fill with bulbs or annuals, and the towering leylandii and beech hedge at the path end form a dramatic entrance with a subtle play of leaf colour and form.

# Shamley Green
*Surrey*

In 1921 a corrugated tin hut, First World War army surplus, was brought from Chilworth Camp to house the growing congregation of a religious sect nicknamed 'Coclers', cocoa being the only recreational beverage they were permitted. Wood frame additions were soon made and the leylandii planted against two sides to camouflage the tin shell and provide a modicum of insulation against the cold. These giant evergreen earmuffs may not be everyone's idea of topiary, but certainly part of the definition of the art includes an inventive use of a clipped hedge.

## Basing
### *Hampshire*

Every village has its memorial cross, but few can claim to have one clipped in yew. Basing village tradition holds that their cross was planted to commemorate Queen Victoria's Jubilee in 1887. But it is more likely that it belongs to the legion of cenotaphs erected to honour the dead of the First World War, a theory given credence by the memory of one resident, whose chronology would give a planting date of 1931.

This village boasts four peacocks, all supposedly planted during the 17th century to commemorate the Siege of Basing House. One can only guess at their real age, yet it is likely that the largest bird, at Old Basing House, was planted first, starting a village fashion which hasn't ended – a fledgling is taking shape in a neighbouring garden. The second largest of the four lost his head to a passing lorry – an unusual victim of the plague of traffic congestion on village streets designed for horse and cart. This one, sometimes mistaken for a rabbit, remains as a well-tended and much-loved landmark, part of a yew hedge which once divided the cottage garden into two plots.

## Chenies Manor
*Buckinghamshire*

Henry VIII came to this Manor, once with Anne Boleyn and baby Elizabeth, and once with Katherine Howard, who unwisely cavorted with her paramour, Thomas Culpeper, while the King was laid up with a gammy leg; his limping ghost can be heard making its way to Katherine's bedroom. But he might be happier if he was to try the gardens on the west side of the house made since the 1950s in the area formerly known as the 'little gardens'. The sunken garden, made in the remains of the original, was inspired by the privy gardens at Hampton Court Palace and has low grassy terraces and clipped box cushions around a central pond. This is separated from the formal topiary garden by a narrow allée of yew and leylandii.

Like the original at Hampton Court, the Chenies sunken garden is seen through a screen. But instead of pleached hornbeam, beech or lime, a simple wooden trellis is used, which also provides a frame for standard umbrella-shaped yews. Ivy is starting its climb up the the trellis and the total effect of this device is an especially pleasing combination of shapes and textures.

Four yew hens sit on nests of box in a small lawn surrounded by borders planted largely with white-flowered herbaceous perennials and shrubs. One hen looks the wrong way; while all her sisters gaze at a statue of Cupid in the centre of the lawn she gazes towards the herb garden. In the flurry of planting, it wasn't noticed that one had been put in backwards. The topiary was rescued from a derelict nursery in Berkshire, having survived the Second World War thanks to the attentions of a gardener who hadn't been told to stop. The south side of the garden is a lime arbour similar to the one at Hatfield. The branches are trained as espaliers and the gaps at the base between the trees are filled with angelica, *Cotoneaster horizontalis* and holly.

## Woolton Hall
*Berkshire*

This topiary is said to be 'tailor-made' because it was created by Miss Dodd's father who owned a tailoring business. He supplied the livery for the servants of the local gentry, and his daughter reckons that he got his inspiration from examples he had seen in the gardens of the large estates. She now lives in the cottage and looks after the topiary with the aid of a neighbour who has been tending it for thirty-two years and who took the job over from his father. A box hedge borders the street side of the garden, and yew is used to form the peacocks, arch and boundary hedge between the kitchen garden area and front lawns.

## Waterdell Park
### *Hertfordshire*

The yew and holly topiary hedge in this garden serves a dual purpose, separating the tennis lawn and shrubbery from the sweeping lawns that spread out before the house, and providing a perfect backdrop for a luxuriant curve of herbaceous border. A great deal of care must be taken when clipping a long sweep of hedge like this. It holds a prominent position in the design of the garden, and any mistake made in clipping, a branch lopped out by mistake or undulations resulting from uneven cutting, would be immediately apparent.

## Dorney Court
### *Berkshire*

The manor house of Dorney, The Island of Bees, dates in part from the 15th century and has passed from father to son in unbroken succession since 1600. The double bank of topiary hedges screening the east front of the house does not, however, share the same antiquity and the present incumbent is somewhat dubious about their value, feeling that the girth of the yew is out of proportion to the house; the hens atop the two sugar loaf shapes either side of the drive are cut off every so often and the hedge receives nothing other than an annual clip at the end of each summer.

## Sudeley Castle
*Gloucestershire*

St Mary's Church is framed by surrounding hedges and cushions of yew and a scrap of bedding survives in the roundel before the west front. But even this is treated with the utmost simplicity: concentric borders of gold and green box edge the outer perimeter and form a plinth at the base of the urn. The greenery of forget-me-nots and tulips complete the garden picture, again without a flower in sight.

The Queen's Garden on the east front of the castle was created during the second half of the 19th century by Emma Dent, who was largely responsible for the restoration of the castle and its grounds. This was once the home of Katherine Parr, Henry VIII's widow, and the quartered beds are modelled on the fragrant knots a Tudor lady might have enjoyed. Both ends of the central axis are marked by domes of yew and the north and south sides are enclosed by yew arbours; *clairvoyées* have been clipped into the sides. Originally the beds were planned to take Victorian bedding schemes, but today are full of scented herbs. Rosemary, sage, wormwood, lavender, marjoram and curry plant, in their myriad tints of green, silvery greys and rust brown with a wide variety of leaf shape, texture and form, and contrasted with the sombre yews and bright lawns, provide year-long interest, perfectly demonstrating what can be achieved with simplicity.

## The Wold Furlong
*Gloucestershire*

Topiary is either loved or hated, few people are ambivalent about it. Planted in the 1920s, this hedge owes its survival to one man whose dream it was one day to cut topiary. Fortunately for him, the friend who bought the house and so acquired the topiary loathed gardening, and gave the aspiring topiarist a free hand. The biggest difficulty was reaching the birds: one held the ladder and then pulled the other out of the hedge at the first few attempts, until a scaffold nine feet tall was built. This was a major breakthrough; the shapes regained their former elegance, and a lifelong ambition was fulfilled.

## Chipping Campden
*Gloucestershire*

As mentioned earlier, privet topiary is slightly unreal. During winter and early spring before the leaves burst forth, it looks as though it is cut from Weetabix or Brillo pads – like these peacocks – and appears distinctly unwell, probably because we expect to see evergreen topiary. The owner of these two birds finds them a big responsibility. As soon as he took possession of the property, the first thing he was asked was, 'How are the birds?', and he now feels he has a civic obligation to tend to their every need, which includes clipping little and often throughout the summer. Another intriguing feature of this garden is the use of a pair of Blue Spruce, *Picea pungens glauca*, to form an arch, achieved by pruning away the lower branches and cutting the arch through the branches where they entwine.

## Painswick Churchyard
*Gloucestershire*

David Verey described this churchyard as 'about the best in England', given its distinction by the combination of table tombs and pedestals with the magnificent collection of yew trees, some of which were planted in 1792. Legend has it that there are no more than ninety-nine trees as the hundredth planted always dies, although the spell has apparently been broken. Churchyard yews seem to attract the best legends: at Fortingall in Perthshire, Scotland there was (and still may be) a yew reputed to be the oldest in Europe – that village is also supposed to be Pontius Pilate's birthplace!

## Miserden Churchyard
*Gloucestershire*

The Saxon remains incorporated into the 19th-century restorations give a clue to the great age of this church. While the yew arch is of course not part of this heritage, it is true that most churchyards, particularly in the west of England, have one or more of this native tree. This may give credence to the belief that early Christians built their churches on pagan holy ground – in England the Druids worshipped the immortal yew – and adopted it as a symbol of the resurrection. It was an old country habit to toss a sprig of yew into the open grave: to quote the fool in *Twelfth Night*, 'My shroud of white, stuck all with Yew'.

## Heywood House Lodge
*Wiltshire*

The severe formality and impassive façade of this nicely proportioned cottage are relieved by the topiary hedge surrounding the garden, and the slight note of whimsey introduced by the tails of the two gatepost-peacocks that almost meet to form an arch over the entrance. A less interesting building can be enlivened by a lavish and consequently dramatic use of topiary, but it would have been a mistake to hide this one's attributes behind too many cakestands or peacocks.

## King's Somborne
*Hampshire*

Children are often given a corner of the garden to call their own, a place in which to grow marigolds, wild strawberries and johnny jump-ups. In 1920 a ten year-old boy was given a small yew tree and he began training it into a topiary specimen with seven tiers representing the days of the week and a cross on top in honour of the church opposite the house. Shortly after the Second World War the bottom disc became diseased and was cut away, but otherwise the tree grew steadily from a short skinny youngster into a twenty-foot adult. Today the topiary is clipped by that little boy's grown-up son. He has been doing it for the past ten years and it took him half that time to become proficient. It is not easy to maintain the straight vertical line of the topiary. The ladder from which he works tends to push the top of the tree out of true. At one time the cross was definitely beginning to list, but a spot of hard pruning and repeated careful scrutiny of the tree from a vantage point across the street helped him to correct the imbalance.

## Norman Chapel
*Gloucestershire*

The conversion of this 11th-century chapel and the creation of its surrounding garden and girdling hedge took place from 1903–05, the work of Charles Ashby for Ananda Coomaraswamy and his wife, Ethel Mairet. Both were members of the group of artist–craftsmen seeking inspiration in the Cotswold countryside, he was a botanical scholar and brought William Morris's printing press to the chapel. Ethel was a weaver, but she also laid out the gardens and presumably was responsible for the topiary hedge. In the course of time some of the figures have disappeared, but as can be seen by the tufts of yew, these with the rest of the garden are being restored.

## Sapperton
*Gloucestershire*

The greatest concentration of topiary in England is undoubtedly in Gloucestershire, with the village of Sapperton and the shade of Ernest Gimson at the epicentre of what was Arts and Crafts Land. Gimson was a student of J. D. Sedding, topiary's great champion, and a partner of the Barnsley Brothers, Ernest and Sidney. Design shockwaves emanated from their workshop–saleroom at Daneway House in Sapperton: Rodmarton Manor (page 37) is one of their greatest achievements and the widespread use of topiary in Cotswold gardens made in the early 1900s is an indication of their influence in all areas of domestic design.

## Austin House
*Gloucestershire*

This magnificent topiary mass, matched by another in the same village, looks like an enormous French poodle, sheared by a Cubist. It towers over the garden, making a breath-taking centrepiece to the design of lawns and box-edged parterre. But its original intention was slightly more down to earth. The yews were planted to screen two privies; its sister obliged for three. No wonder they grew so splendidly – how could they not?

## Barnsley House
*Gloucestershire*

In her book *The Scented Garden*, Rosemary Verey described the plants most suitable for making a knot garden based on the experience of creating her own, shown here: 'box, in variety; *Teucrium chamaedrys*, or wall germander as it was called in Elizabethan times, and cotton lavender . . . Phillyrea is good for clipping and is admirable for a mound at the centre of the knot.' The rosemary hedge around the knot is gone, but the 'four fat men' of variegated holly remain. She recommends tracing the knot lines in sand on to the site and then planting with slips or rooted cuttings in spring. Note how the threads are clipped to varying levels giving the appearance of being woven.

# Gatacre Park
## *Warwickshire*

Lady Thompson's father was a keen topiarist; when he moved from Worcestershire to the family home near Gatacre he brought along his favourite box topiary, which was already advanced in years when he acquired it. He continued to create *cabinets de verdure*, arbours and other vegetable sculptures, instilling in his daughter the purist line: frames were not allowed and all topiary had to be created by eye, although string could be used to tie two branches together to form a teapot handle or other curve.

The fifteen topiary figures ranged along a terrace walk below the south front of Gatacre Park have been planted over the last fifty-seven years by one family. All the trees were self-sown yew seedlings found within the grounds. They were grown on to small bushes and then moved to permanent sites, at which point Sir Edward and Lady Thompson stood back and considered what could be made of them: 'rather like doodling'. The results are his and her teddy bears (his has eyeholes which are given orbs of blue thistle heads in summer), two corkscrews, the 1930s cartoon character 'Flook' that looks like a cross between Woody Woodpecker and the Roadrunner, a pedestal with a knob where a Queen Mary would have been but for a gardener who was unaware of Lady Thompson's ambition, and a teapot started ten years ago.

The little sunken garden, still known as the New Garden although it was made in 1935, is entered through an arch clipped from yew, and each corner of the pool is marked by single specimens of *Taxus baccata* 'Fastigata', which give dramatic emphasis to the ascending vista.

Two grass tennis courts once occupied the lawns on the east front of the house, and this was the sitting out area, framed by cool green obelisks of yew. Elsewhere in the garden there is a large yew hedge which Sir Edward feels may be contemporary with the Elizabethan house that originally stood on the site. It was demolished in 1850, and the present house was built in its place.

The Gatacre Monster was a shaggy golden yew when the Thompsons first came to Gatacre in 1930. They tried to turn it into a sitting hen, but were not all that successful and it became the curious object we see today, the survivor of several batterings by coachloads of visiting garden lovers.

## Cross
*Somerset*

Mr Smith's great-grandfather planted four of these six topiary spires soon after he moved into the cottage in 1842; it is not known when the other topiary was added. A photograph from the family album dated 1895 shows the original four as being very spindly and only about eight feet tall. It's a rare treat to find cottage garden topiary so well documented, and usually only happens when it has been in the continuous possession of one family. Today, the spires are fifteen feet tall, with the two nearest the road five feet taller, and they have a notoriety to match their height, attracting busloads of tourists and trippers from nearby Bristol. The peak of the rubbernecking season coincides with the end-of-summer topiary shearing, prolonging Mr Smith's labour of love as he downs electric clippers to answer questions.

## Ings
*Cumbria*

This topiary has been saved by a true devotee of the art. When the Burtons took on the garden the shapes had been lost but by tracing the stronger growing twigs Mr Burton was able to resurrect some of the original designs. The others he made up as he went along until inspiration ran out: he'd used up quite a bit in his previous garden where there was a perfect Scottie dog, peacock, basket, Loch Ness monster, a wonky llama and a lamp-post just beginning to take shape. The new garden's topiary is of box and yew and they are clipped in that order beginning at the end of June.

## Lake Coniston
*Cumbria*

'And where some further licence is permitted, we may group our clipped yews, uniting them in single arches, open cages, cross hoops, pagodas, and terminate them with a finial of bird or beast, such as used to adorn the stone gables and oak stair-newels of the early Stuarts. Grown out of the natural tree, these shapely forms elude the restrictions of our artificial scale, and look well whatever their size or bulk. The giant sentinels at the cottage gate do not dwarf the low whitewashed walls' so wrote Walter Godfrey in his book *Gardens in the Making*. The giant green sentinels here would seem to disprove his theory of form and scale, and make even a substantial house into one fit only for dolls.

# Peover Hall
*Cheshire*

In the northern corner of the garden, approached along a double avenue of young limes, lies the Theatre Garden. It was created *c.*1930, but became overgrown and neglected during the war years, when the house was abandoned. The Brookes have most recently been restoring this area, planting the lime avenues and renovating or replanting damaged yews. The small wooden house was moved from another part of the garden to give focus to the area, and is referred to as The Temple, a refuge for croquet mallets, cricket bats and a small boy on rainy days. Young Master Brooke is proud of his garden and conducts an exemplary tour; he likes gardens because the colours make him cheerful, and the pink garden is one of his favourite areas for the wild strawberries growing there.

Bowler hats and low hedges of box mark the beds in the white garden. This tranquil enclosure is planted with white and cream-coloured roses, delphiniums, viburnum, philadelphus, tulips, lilac, artemisia and lily-of-the-valley. Beyond this is a garden of pink climbing roses underplanted with wild strawberries. The walled gardens were made in what was the 17th-century kitchen garden, and a walk amidst the perfumed flowers serenaded by the hum of bees is to step back in time into an Elizabethan garden.

Topiary figures abound in the lily pond garden. Yew spirals are ranged before a colonnaded seating area along one side, and yew hens sit at opposite ends of the pool. Crenellated yew hedges and a brick wall supported by yew buttresses *à la* Arley Hall (see page 6) complete the enclosure. The yews are clipped once a year by a team of three gardeners and are mulched throughout the summer with lawn clippings. The only fertiliser they receive is what is put on nearby flower beds.

Over the past thirty years the Tudor hall, built in 1585, and surrounding gardens have been restored by the Brooke family. Much of the remaining land had been made into a landscape park around 1760, designed by William Eames. The walled garden areas shown here were laid out *c.*1880 when most of the topiary and hedges were planted. These hedges divide the space into six interconnected garden rooms, each with its special quality. The crossing paths in the rectangular rose garden, divide this area into quarters. Old shrub roses are the favourite throughout the garden and the high yew hedges help to contain their perfume. Small portholes and an arch cut through the hedge 'with knobs on' give access to the herb garden.

## Martley
*Worcestershire*

The Norman church of St Peter may well have been built on the site of an Anglo-Saxon building, as the parish of Martley is one of the oldest in Worcestershire. There are two yew crosses in the churchyard and when and why they were planted no one is certain, but they belong to the great tradition of churchyard topiary. A yew at Swallowfield in Berkshire was credited with being older than its 13th-century church, and Harlington churchyard in Bedfordshire had a yew which had been clipped during the 18th century to form an enormous canopy ten feet from the ground; a verse about it recalls:

'So thick, so fine, so full, so wide
A troop of guards might under it ride.
A weathercock who gaped to crow it,
This world is mine and all below it.'

## Wenlock Priory
*Cheshire*

Often the charm of a topiary garden lies in the incongruity of its setting, and few things could be more startling than to find a collection of teddy bears and hens in the stately ruins of a Cluniac priory. The property was acquired during the 19th century by the Motley family who set about creating a garden, using the 12th-century chapter house arcading as a backdrop. Some of the topiary is made by planting a ring of green yew trees around a single golden yew. The green was clipped to make the base and the golden brought up to become a teddy or hen.

## Ayhill
*Herefordshire*

Growing from a low yew hedge, the two topiary umbrellas mark the division between the kitchen garden and the flower garden in front of a 400-year-old thatched cottage. At the end nearest the house, one tree has been left to assume its natural shape as if to illustrate William Robinson's argument that the best 'vegetable sculpture' is a tree grown naturally, not one that has been disciplined by the shears of the topiarist.

## New House
*Herefordshire*

It is thought that the two topiary 'bowers' in this farmhouse garden are at least 100 years old. They are more than just decorative features and have served as sheds where the garden-help stored their tools and sheltered from the rain, and later as cavalry forts, then army command tents as children battled across the garden. Jeff, who tends them today for Mr and Mrs Pudge, the fourth generation of the family to live in New House, took over from his father who had worked with Grandfather Pudge to create not just the bowers, but peacocks, hens in baskets and other topiary in his own as well as the 'guv'nor's' garden. Of his father's skill Jeff says, 'He'd see it growin' and growin' and think could I make summat else to that . . . and I sort of picked it up.'

## Birtsmorton Court
*Cheshire*

The long rectangular garden is separated from the 12th-century fortified manor by a moat and bounded at one end by the Westminster Pool, created by Henry VII to mark the consecration of Westminster Abbey. This is balanced at the opposite end by a pool of lawn enclosed by topiary hedges. Eight pairs of box and ball yew topiary form an avenue down one side of a plain square of lawn. The hedges on the remaining three sides are between ten and fifteen feet tall and screen the long herbaceous borders which run along the surrounding brick wall. This garden may have a disarmingly simple layout but its effect, thanks to the mass of topiary, is wildly extravagant.

## Hill Court
*Herefordshire*

In 1698 Richard Clarke began work on the house and gardens of Hill Court, but the topiary walk and sundial court were laid out in the last half of the 19th century. Before the Second World War the sundial court was a formal flower garden and each pyramid was paired with a box-edged circular bed. An annotated plan of the period records, 'The pattern [of the bedding] was repeated four times. The planting was always tulips and forget-me-nots in the spring and either stocks with a clump of cherry-pie in the middle or antirrhinums in the summer. During the war beetroot and carrots were grown.' Beyond the ornamental gates lies the topiary walk.

*Clairvoyées*, window-like openings in hedge or wall, were an extremely effective device for focussing attention on a distant view, at the same time as giving it dramatic emphasis. The element of surprise is important to a successful garden scheme, and it does make you gasp when a solid wall of greenery suddenly gives way to a knee-trembling vista. This lack of surprise in Brown's (and others') landscapes contributed to their fall from grace. In 1772 William Chambers wrote that when viewing a landscape garden all was immediately revealed: 'he sees nothing to amuse him, nothing to excite his curiosity, nor anything to keep up his attention.'

The yews in the topiary walk are over 110 years old and more than seven feet in height. The entrance to the walk leads off the main axis and is marked by topiary peacocks. Opposite, another path leads into an open area with beds outlined in clipped box. It was planned that the marvellous view of Goodrich Castle should be enjoyed from this walk, so at intervals along the passage the trees are trained to form small arbours opposite *clairvoyées* which frame the view of the castle.

## Potash Farm
*Suffolk*

Spirals have always had a reputation for being the most difficult topiary shape to achieve satisfactorily. Miles Hadfield wrote that the tree is kept to a single shoot and then wound around a stake. Side shoots are allowed to grow out from the twisting trunk, and clipped to emphasise the spiral. Box can be treated in like fashion to make a miniature corkscrew. However, most spirals seem to rely on the steady eye and hand of the clipper to carve the branches into a spiral growing from a straight trunk.

## Rishangles
*Suffolk*

Geometric shapes can be combined to form some unusual topiary figures. Such styling was most popular during the 1890s and a close examination of the garden plans illustrated in Sedding's book *Garden-Craft Old and New* shows topiary features similar in outline to these tops of clipped green and gold yew in a Suffolk churchyard, spinning between the headstones.

# Swannington Manor
## *Norfolk*

The whens and wherefores of this incredible topiary hedge are lost in the mists of time, but it is at least 300 years old and contemporary with the date of the house. The hedge is made of green and gold forms of yew and box and two types of holly. Clipping begins in August and takes three months to complete. Each year the hedge is given a substantial dose of general purpose fertiliser. The trees are arranged in parallel rows and this indicates that the hedge may be the remnants of an arbour that once skirted the outer perimeter of the pleasure garden; it is possible to walk inside the entire length of each hedge.

The newest addition to the Swannington Manor gardens is this modern interpretation of an Elizabethan knot garden, shown here at eighteen months old. It has been laid out where once there was lawn. To prepare the plot, the grass was sprayed with a herbicide and then rotovated and the planting lines for the dwarf box hedges marked out in lime. The hearts in the middle knot are infilled with creeping thyme, but the rest of the pattern is picked out in two different colours of gravel. Pot-grown topiary specimens flank the knots and the bed along the opposite side is filled with herbs. Even in its youth a knot garden makes a pretty garden picture.

## Aylsham
*Norfolk*

The lady of the house thinks that somewhere in this enormous yew hedge there is a peacock. One of the things about topiary and formal hedges is the way their character changes as they grow; the bushes may remain beautifully turned out, but they have in fact burst their seams. Looking through old gardening books and magazines, one frequently encounters fifty-year-old (and older) photographs and engravings showing a famous garden in its youth before the peacocks turned to queer shaped blobs of box and the graceful line of yew hedge began to look like the fat lady at the circus.

## Costessey
*Norfolk*

Thirty-one years ago the yew which forms this topiary was obscuring the drive leading up to the house and something had to be done. Not wishing to grub up the tree, Mr Gunton hit upon topiary; he had always admired the topiary he had seen and the growth of the problem tree seemed to mimic the crenellations and finials adorning the house. And so it developed, although the central finial is gaining in stature since it is so difficult to reach when the tree is being clipped.

## Parnham House
*Dorset*

The formal yew terrace set before the Elizabethan manor house was laid out *c*.1909, and is the work of either Harold Peto or Inigo Thomas, both of whom carried out commissions at neighbouring houses around that time. The garden carries the hallmarks of both their styles; Peto was particularly successful working with water in his schemes, and the yews at Parnham are intersected by water rills which feed into a cascade at the bottom of the terrace. Thomas, who designed the gardens at Athelhampton, used clipped yew to create formal settings of great serenity to set off the elaborate architecture of the houses where he worked. At Parnham there are two squares of 25 cone-shaped yew. When the Makepeaces came to the house ten years ago, the yews had lost their definition and, to restore them accurately, a traditional wooden template was cut using the dimensions of the best tree. This is put against the trees to provide an accurate cutting line. Flooding from the water channels and the slightly acid soil had severely damaged several trees, and these are now replaced.

## Oaksmere
*Suffolk*

More East Anglian fantasies, this in the garden of the 16th-century dower house to Brome Hall, seat of the Cornwallis family (who surrendered the American colonies) and known in its heyday as the 'Versailles of England'. Eighty-one pieces of yew topiary remain and are about two hundred years old. The group of seven standing apart from the main collection have become known as the Seven Sisters as they were supposedly planted to represent the seven daughters of the family standing together with arms linked.

## Corscombe
*Dorset*

When the Fieldings moved into this house thirty-three years ago, the box trees were tiny bushes. As they grew it occurred to Mrs Fielding how nice they would look clipped into tidy shapes. As is so often the case with new topiary, the spirals, 'whirly bits' as she calls them, suggested themselves. The five shapes are clipped twice, once in the spring and again in the autumn. The only feed they receive is from the farmyard manure spread on the flowerbeds at their feet.

## East Lambrook
*Somerset*

In small cottage gardens such as this the addictive nature of topiary is revealed, and what begins as a simple experiment of putting lollipops on top of a privet hedge leads eventually to a collection of peacocks and cakestands in yew and box. Once these are established, the floodgates of personal expression are thrown open and embellishments, like the small thatched birdhouse below the largest peacock, are ad libbed, giving expression to the gardener's highly individual vision of paradise.

## Stancombe Park
*Gloucestershire*

The box topiary hedge was planted at the beginning of the last century when the Folly garden and Temple at Stancombe Park were created. It forms an integral part of this garden, completely enclosing it and thereby establishing a *giardino segreto* – with a purpose. Situated well away from the house and approached through a forest of laurel, it was supposedly created by a clergyman as a trysting place where he could meet his lover without his wife's knowledge.

## Bewley Common
*Wiltshire*

Next to geometric shapes it is most difficult to make a recognisable animal shape, unless you choose one that has a characteristic outline. At Nymans there is a pair of sleeping lions either side of an entrance to the walled garden, and there is also a pair at the centre of the Hatfield Maze, but you do have to be told what they are; there is no 'signature' to the shape. This is why birds are so popular: it is easy to see rudimentary wings and tailfeathers in arching branches of yew and box. Teddy bear shapes, like those at Gatacre, are more successful, as is this yew rabbit, because we know immediately that something with long ears has just got to be a bunny!

## Debenhams
*London*

The appeal of topiary has a broad base. When this long-established department store re-opened in the spring after extensive modernisation, and with its vast windows displaying formal fashion, the display manager hit upon topiary to set the theme. Originally it was meant to be temporary, but has been so successful that the trees have been re-made in a better quality material than the original plastic. They will come down for Christmas, but go back in place when spring arrives. He remarked that in the United States, topiary display is extremely popular and the range of materials and shapes extensive, particularly from sources in California. This is intriguing; in American gardens the love of genuine topiary has never faded and garden designers have made wide use of it in their schemes, extending the frontiers of the art. The work of Thomas D. Church illustrates this. In his own garden he trained vines into lattice patterns, removing the foliage when the stems had thickened, and clipped away the underskirts of box trees, exposing the gnarled trunks and clipping the foliage into pompons at the ends of the branches.

## Paignton
*Devon*

Forty years ago, Mr Norman planted his first topiary, and as the first four small examples grew they seemed to be out of proportion to their setting. So he planted a few more bushes on the other side to grow over the garage entrance, and began clipping them into the collection of dogs and cats we see today. What is particularly appealing about this topiary is the feeling of movement given by the way the animals are set on their base – at slightly varying angles instead of the usual neat line. The ducks, too, seem to be revolving on the wheel of a funfair shooting gallery. Topiary such as this really deserves to be exhibited, if it were possible, in galleries and museums, with the finest examples of English Folk Art.

## Tyler's Green
*West Sussex*

The usual purpose for planting a hedge is to provide a screen and certainly that was the intention when this splendid yew hedge was installed. But rather than leave it as a bare wall of sombre green, the top growth was trained into arches behind which the house is cloistered. Such uniform undulations would be best formed by tying the young shoots to canes or wires, each with the same degree of curve.

## Quinton
*West Midlands*

It seems that topiary shapes most often suggest themselves. Some people do use frames or clip according to a sketched design, especially for geometric shapes, but zoomorphic topiary is almost always the result of on-the-spot inspiration – it just started to look like a giraffe. Old Nessie, as this hedge is lovingly known, is a good example, and there are a number of other Nessies dotted around England, inspired by the natural hummocky growth of box bushes – and the Loch Ness Monster.

## Great Cheverell
*Wiltshire*

This elegant Queen Anne manor house rests securely in its cushion of history, between a 13th-century church and diminutive magistrates court house, the interior of which is a perfect octagonal room. But the beauty and curiosity of the place do not end with the architecture. The massive hedge undulating along the slope is, like the hedge at Swannington Manor (see page 74), a mix of yew and box. Fifteen years ago a fire destroyed part of the hedge and Brigadier Oliver Brooke sought advice from a retired forestry officer. By counting the rings he was able to say the trees were at least 450 years old, and also gave the probable reason for the hedge's bumpy outline: the only other hedge he knew of like it was in Yorkshire and had been used by nuns to dry linen sheets, and the weight of the wet washing spread across the branches had 'trained' the growth of the bushes.

At a right angle to the 'laundry' hedge, a superb topiary hedge gives shelter to the garden and an ancient mulberry tree. The hedge may have been planted in the late 1800s since the trees were well established when, about 1910, the gardener decided the peacocks were facing the wrong way – into the garden rather than towards the view – and began the painstaking work of turning them around, which process took six years. When Brigadier and Mrs Brooke arrived in 1961, the same gardener was tending the hedge and he proudly told them of his achievement. Today all the topiary is clipped in August, but the steep slopes on which the hedges are planted make it too difficult to mulch with manure.

## Rampisham
*Dorset*

This is New Wave Topiary – an interpretation for the 21st century of the oldest gardening art. It combines the structural traditions of the past (the bed and chair as training frames) with a fast growing plant material (grass) to provide topiary for the modern instant garden. The form of the sleeping man was made by moulding chicken wire over the model and then lining it with a water-retentive material. The seed was sown just as for a lawn and the grass regularly clipped once it was established. Regular applications of lawn fertiliser and occasional hand-weeding keep it looking tip-top. It is reminiscent of the earthenware heads that appear around St Patrick's Day; watered daily, they sprout green-grass hair – ideal table-top topiary.

## Bewley Common
*Wiltshire*

Fred the Dog is rather more low key than Rabbit (see page 147), relying on his natural beauty to make an impression. Fred is cut from hawthorn and each spring bursts forth into snowy white blossom to bid farewell to winter. Fred and Rabbit are what topiary is really all about – it is fun, it always has been and it always will be. Even in its most architectural guise there is something faintly 'tee-hee' about it – pyramids made of box or summerhouses clipped in yew are beautiful no doubt, but they are made to amuse, to make one say, 'Oh, Gosh!'.

# PHOTOGRAPHER'S NOTES

*'A mighty maze: but not without a plan.'* Pope

First make your plan. How do you contrive to be in over sixty gardens throughout England at the moment when the topiary is at its best and produce over 135 pictures of hedges without subjecting your viewer to page after page of unvarying greenery?

Photographing topiary is unlike other garden photography in that it is such a specific subject. One can usually find something to photograph in most gardens given the prevailing conditions, but photographing topiary is like photographing a sundial and it is often intended to be seen from a particular viewpoint. Hedges take the light differently according to their variety. Yew can look wonderful in winter with a strong back light; it can virtually disappear when lit from the front until it develops its yellow summer growth, when it shimmers in all lights. Box is almost iridescent in midsummer under the black sky of a thunderstorm.

We started in January and ended in June, travelling from south to north to try to keep up with the growth rate. Clipping time differs for yew, box and privet which further complicated the itinerary. Gardens can look very bleak in the depths of winter, although dawn with the frost hard on the ground is a magical time for photographing topiary. Snow transforms everything, but it was already thawing by the time I had dug myself out of Dorset this particular winter.

A well-researched programme will take you to the better known gardens when the topiary is looking its best, but be prepared for the rare excitement of a sudden discovery of roadside topiary and for its remarkable effects on the driver. Not to mention tantalising phantom topiary to which one would be directed by a reliable source, only to find that it was given the chop years ago.

To cope with the speed at which it was sometimes necessary to work (at times it was more like sports photography) and to maximise on optical variety, I used Nikon cameras and lenses covering 20 mm, 24 mm, 28 mm P.C. (to keep verticals upright when shooting from above or below), 35 mm, 55 mm and a 70–200 mm zoom for tighter framing. Warming filters 81 A, B and C were used as were polarising filters, which not only increase drama in the sky, especially when used with a neutral density graduated filter, but also have a remarkable effect on foliage by removing the shine on the surface of leaves so making them look greener. Rooftops, ladders, bedroom windows, and on one occasion a hundred foot folly provided a variety of vertiginous camera angles.

With the exception of Selina, the fire-eater of Biddulph Grange (see page 58), who was shot on Fuji 50 as she left me no time to bracket exposures, Kodachrome 25 Professional film was used throughout, being the sharpest 35 mm reversal film I know. A tripod and cable release were always necessary to deal with its slow speed, the additional filtration and the small apertures used. The other essential items of equipment proved to be a compass (to establish the direction of the sun) and a pair of gumboots.

As well as wishing to thank all those topiarists whose masterworks appear in this book, I would like to apologise to all those who eluded us: they must be out there somewhere.

My special thanks to Lal Hitchcock and Ruby Wright.

GEORGE WRIGHT
September 1987

# FURTHER READING

Aslet, Clive, *The Last Country Houses*, 1982, Yale University Press, USA

Baker, Margaret, *Discovering Topiary*, 1969, Shire Publications, Tring, Hertfordshire

Blomfield, Sir Reginald, *The Formal Garden in England*, 1st ed. 1892, reprinted 1985, Waterstone & Co Ltd, London

Church, Thomas D., *Gardens Are For People*, 2nd ed. 1983 McGraw Hill, New York

Curtis, C. H., *The Book of Topiary*, 1904, Bodley Head, London

Desmond, Ray, *The Bibliography of British Gardens*, 1984, St Paul's Bibliographies, London. For *Country Life* listings

Flint, Harrison L., 'Boxwood', *Horticulture*, Vol LXV, no. 3, p 51–59, 1987, Boston

Godfrey, Walter, *Gardens in the Making*, 1914, London

Gradidge, Roderick, *Dream Houses*, 1980, Constable & Co, London

Hadfield, Miles, *Topiary and Ornamental Hedges*, 1971, A&C Black, London

Jellicoe, Sir Geoffrey and Susan, ed. *The Oxford Companion to Gardens*, 1986, Oxford University Press, Oxford

Lawson, William, *The Countrie Housewifes Garden*, 1st ed. 1617

Lloyd, Christoper, *The Adventurous Gardener*, 1983, Allen Lane, London

Lloyd, Nathaniel, *Garden Craftsmanship in Yew and Box*, 1925, Ernest Benn Ltd, London

Masson, Georgina, *Italian Gardens*, 1961, Thames & Hudson, London

Mountaine, Dydymus (syn. Thomas Hill), *The Gardeners Labyrinth*, 1577

Muthesius, Hermann, *The English House*, 1st ed. 1904, translated Janet Seligman, 1979, Granada, London

Robinson, William, *Garden Design and Architect's Gardens*, 1892, John Murrey, London

Scott, H. Baillie, *Houses and Gardens*, 1933, Beresford Press, London

Sedding, J.D., *Garden Craft Old and New*, 1891, Kegan Paul, Trench, Trubner & Co Ltd, London

Stewart, Cecil, *Topiary*, 1954, Golden Cockerel Press

Strong, Sir Roy, *The Renaissance Garden in England*, 1979, Thames & Hudson, London

Thomas, Graham Stuart, *Gardens of the National Trust*, 1979, Weidenfeld & Nicolson, London

Triggs, H. Inigo, *Garden Craft in Europe, 1913*, B. T. Batsford, London

Verey, Rosemary and Alvilde Lees Milne. *The Englishwoman's Garden*, 1980, Chatto & Windus, London

Wharton, Edith, *Italian Villas and their Gardens*, 1904, Century Co, New York

# INDEX

Page numbers in *italics* refer to illustrations